Let's Go
giraffe
초등 필수 영단어
따라 쓰기 900

# Let's Go
# 초등 필수 영단어 따라 쓰기 900

**저 자** 이민정, 장현애
**발행인** 고본화
**발 행** 반석출판사
2022년 1월 10일 초판 3쇄 인쇄
2022년 1월 15일 초판 3쇄 발행
**홈페이지** www.bansok.co.kr
**이메일** bansok@bansok.co.kr
**블로그** blog.naver.com/bansokbooks

07547 서울시 강서구 양천로 583. B동 1007호
(서울시 강서구 염창동 240-21번지 우림블루나인 비즈니스센터 B동 1007호)
**대표전화** 02) 2093-3399 **팩 스** 02) 2093-3393
**출 판 부** 02) 2093-3395 **영업부** 02) 2093-3396
**등록번호** 제315-2008-000033호



ISBN 978-89-7172-894-9 (13740)

반석출판사
Bansok

# 머리말

요새는 영어를 잘하는 친구들이 많은 것 같아요. 영어를 잘하는 친구들을 보면 대부분 단어를 많이 알고 있어요. 단어를 많이 알아야 말도 할 수 있고 쓸 수도 있으니까요.

단어는 눈으로 보면서 외울 수도 있지만, 손으로 쓰면서 외우면 좀 더 오래 기억할 수 있다는 거 아세요? 그래서 쓰면서 단어를 공부할 수 있는 책이 나왔어요. 그런데 그냥 글만 있으면 공부가 재미없잖아요? 그래서 친구들이 그림을 보면서 즐겁게 단어를 쓰고 외울 수 있도록 재미있게 공부할 수 있는 책이 나왔어요.

철자는 쓰고, 발음은 읽으면서 공부할 수 있도록 한글 발음도 함께 써 놓았으니 친구들이 좀 더 쉽게 영어 단어 공부를 할 수 있을 거예요. 하루 분량의 단어 쓰기 공부가 끝나면 단어 한글 뜻과 영단어가 함께 녹음되어 있는 mp3 파일을 들으면서 복습해 보세요. 머리에 아주 오랫동안 남을 거예요.

5일치 공부가 끝나면 연습문제를 풀어 보세요. 그동안 공부한 것을 얼마나 기억하고 있는지 테스트할 수 있어요. 연습문제는 다양한 스타일로 이루어져 있어 복습도 지루하지 않아요.

그럼 즐거운 영단어 쓰기 공부를 하러 떠나 볼까요?

# 목차

# 알파벳 쓰기

| | |
|---|---|
| A a | A<br>a |
| B b | B<br>b |
| C c | C<br>c |
| D d | D<br>d |
| E e | E<br>e |
| F f | F<br>f |
| G g | G<br>g |
| H h | H<br>h |

| | |
|---|---|
| I i | I<br>i |
| J j | J<br>j |
| K k | K<br>k |
| L l | L<br>l |
| M m | M<br>m |
| N n | N<br>n |
| O o | O<br>o |
| P p | P<br>p |

# 알파벳 쓰기

| | |
|---|---|
| Q q | Q<br>q |
| R r | R<br>r |
| S s | S<br>s |
| T t | T<br>t |
| U u | U<br>u |
| V v | V<br>v |
| W w | W<br>w |
| X x | X<br>x |

| Y y | Y |
| --- | --- |
| | y |
| Z z | Z |
| | z |

# 알파벳 대문자 쓰기

START

A

FINISH

a

# 01 성별, 노소 / 가족

|  |  |
|---|---|
|  여자<br>woman<br>워먼 | woman |
|  남자<br>man<br>맨 | man |
|  노인<br>elderly person<br>앨들리 펄슨 | elderly person |
|  소년<br>boy<br>보이 | boy |
|  소녀<br>girl<br>걸 | girl |
|  청소년<br>adolescent<br>애들레슨트 | adolescent |
|  어린이<br>child<br>차일드 | child |
|  아기<br>baby<br>베이비 | baby |

| | | |
|---|---|---|
|  | 아버지(아빠)<br>father, dad<br>파더, 댇 | father, dad |
|  | 어머니(엄마)<br>mother, mom<br>마더, 맘 | mother, mom |
|  | 언니/누나<br>elder sister<br>엘더 시스터 | elder sister |
|  | 오빠/형<br>elder brother<br>엘더 브라더 | elder brother |
|  | 남동생<br>younger brother<br>영거 브라더 | younger brother |
|  | 여동생<br>younger sister<br>영거 시스터 | younger sister |
|  | 아들<br>son<br>썬 | son |
|  | 딸<br>daughter<br>도러 | daughter |

DAY 02

# 친가 / 외가

| | | |
|---|---|---|
| | 친할아버지<br>paternal grandfather<br>퍼터널 그랜파더 | paternal grandfather |
| | 친할머니<br>paternal grandmother<br>퍼터널 그랜마더 | paternal grandmother |
| | 고모<br>aunt<br>앤트 | aunt |
| | 고모부<br>uncle<br>엉클 | uncle |
| | 큰아버지/작은아버지(삼촌)<br>uncle<br>엉클 | uncle |
| | 큰어머니/숙모<br>aunt<br>앤트 | aunt |
| | 사촌형/사촌오빠/사촌남동생<br>cousin<br>커즌 | cousin |
| | 사촌누나/사촌언니/사촌여동생<br>cousin<br>커즌 | cousin |

| | | |
|---|---|---|
|  | 외할아버지<br>maternal grandfather<br>머터널 그랜파더 | maternal grandfather |
|  | 외할머니<br>maternal grandmother<br>머터널 그랜마더 | maternal grandmother |
|  | 외삼촌<br>uncle<br>엉클 | uncle |
|  | 외숙모<br>aunt<br>앤트 | aunt |
|  | 이모<br>aunt<br>앤트 | aunt |
|  | 이모부<br>uncle<br>엉클 | uncle |
|  | 사촌형/사촌오빠/사촌 남동생<br>cousin<br>커즌 | cousin |
|  | 사촌누나/사촌언니/사촌여동생<br>cousin<br>커즌 | cousin |

DAY 03

# 직업 I

| | |
|---|---|
|  간호사<br>nurse<br>널스 | nurse |
|  약사<br>pharmacist<br>파머씨스트 | pharmacist |
|  의사<br>doctor<br>닥터 | doctor |
|  선생님/교사<br>teacher<br>티쳐 | teacher |
|  교수<br>professor<br>프로페써 | professor |
|  가수<br>singer<br>씽어 | singer |
|  음악가<br>musician<br>뮤지션 | musician |
|  화가<br>painter<br>페인터 | painter |

공무원
civil servant
씨빌 써번트

civil servant

요리사
cook
쿡

cook

소방관
fire fighter
파이어 파이터

fire fighter

승무원
flight attendant
플라잇 어텐던트

flight attendant

판사
judge
져지

judge

검사
prosecutor
프로씨큐터

prosecutor

변호사
lawyer
러여

lawyer

사업가
businessman
비즈니스맨

businessman

DAY 04

# 직업 II

| | | |
|---|---|---|
|  | 회사원<br>company employee<br>컴퍼니 임플로이 | company employee |
|  | 학생<br>student<br>스튜든트 | student |
|  | 농부<br>farmer<br>파머 | farmer |
|  | 작가<br>writer<br>라이러 | writer |
|  | 정치가<br>politician<br>폴리티션 | politician |
|  | 미용사<br>hairdresser<br>헤어드레서 | hairdresser |
|  | 군인<br>soldier<br>솔져 | soldier |
|  | 경찰관<br>police officer<br>폴리스 오피서 | police officer |

| | | |
|---|---|---|
| 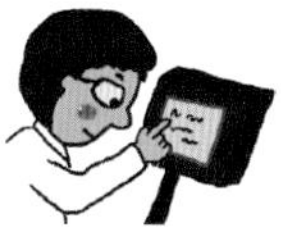 | 엔지니어<br>engineer<br>엔지니어 | engineer |
|  | 통역원<br>interpreter<br>인터프리터 | interpreter |
|  | 비서<br>secretary<br>쎄크리터리 | secretary |
|  | 회계사<br>accountant<br>어카운턴트 | accountant |
|  | 수의사<br>veterinarian<br>베터내리언 | veterinarian |
|  | 건축가<br>architect<br>아키텍트 | architect |
|  | 편집자<br>editor<br>에디터 | editor |
|  | 운동선수<br>athlete<br>애쓸릿 | athlete |

DAY 05

# 성격

명랑한
cheerful
취어풀

cheerful

상냥한
tender
텐더

tender

친절한
kind
카인드

kind

당당한
confident
컨피던트

confident

대범한
free-hearted
프리허디드

free-hearted

눈치가 빠른
ready-witted
레디위디드

ready-witted

솔직한
straightforward
스트레잇포워드

straightforward

적극적인
active
액티브

active

사교적인
sociable
쏘셔블

sociable

겁이 많은
cowardly
카워들리

cowardly

긍정적인
positive
파저티브

positive

부정적인
negative
네거티브

negative

다혈질인
hot-tempered
핫템퍼드

hot-tempered

냉정한
cold
코울드

cold

내성적인
introverted
인트로버티드

introverted

외향적인
extroverted
엑스트로버티드

extroverted

# 연습문제A

영어단어에 알맞은 뜻을 연결해 보세요.

| | |
|---|---|
| 1. woman | ⓐ 어린이 |
| 2. man | ⓑ 청소년 |
| 3. elderly person | ⓒ 남자 |
| 4. child | ⓓ 여자 |
| 5. boy | ⓔ 노인 |
| 6. girl | ⓕ 소년 |
| 7. adolescent | ⓖ 사촌형 |
| 8. cousin | ⓗ 소녀 |
| 9. doctor | ⓘ 군인 |
| 10. active | ⓙ 고모부 |
| 11. soldier | ⓚ 의사 |
| 12. athlete | ⓛ 적극적인 |
| 13. uncle | ⓜ 운동선수 |
| 14. student | ⓝ 학생 |
| 15. aunt | ⓞ 내성적인 |
| 16. introverted | ⓟ 이모 |

답 1.ⓓ 2.ⓒ 3.ⓔ 4.ⓐ 5.ⓕ 6.ⓗ 7.ⓑ 8.ⓖ 9.ⓚ 10.ⓛ 11.ⓘ 12.ⓜ 13.ⓙ 14.ⓝ 15.ⓟ 16.ⓞ

## 연습문제B

빈칸에 알맞은 단어를 넣어보세요.

**1**

A: 어머니의 직업은 무엇인가요?

What's your mother's job?

왓츠 유어 마더스 잡

B: 엄마는 작가이십니다.

She is a ____________.

쉬 이즈 어 라이러

**2**

A: 장래희망이 뭔가요?

What do you want to be?

왓 두 유 원투 비

B: 저는 선생님이 되고 싶어요.

I want to be a ______________.

아이 원투 비 어 티처

**3**

A: 가족이 몇 명이에요?

How many people are there in your family?

하우 매니 피플 아 데어 인 유어 패밀리

B: 네 명이에요. 아빠, 엄마, 형(오빠), 그리고 저요.

There are four in my family. Father, mother, _______ _________, and me.

데어 아 포 인 마이 패밀리 파더 마더 엘더 브라더 앤 미

**4**

A: 성격이 어떠세요?

What kind of personality do you have?

왓 카인덥 퍼스낼러티 두 유 해브

B: 저는 명랑해요.

I am ______________.

아이 앰 취어풀

답 1. writer 2. teacher 3. elder brother 4. cheerful

DAY 06

# 신체명 I

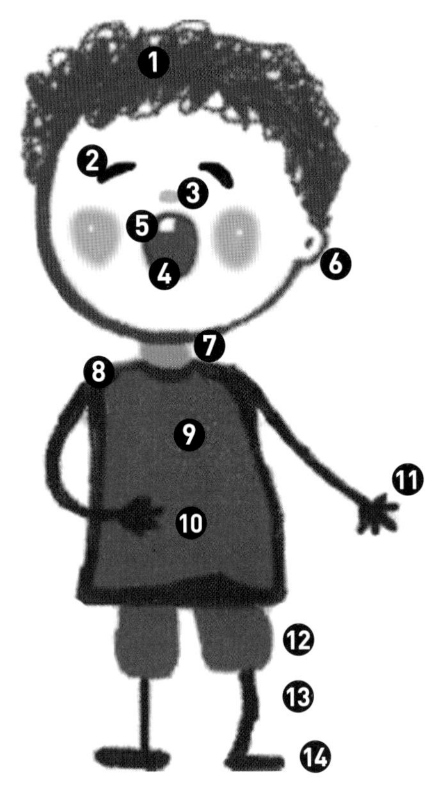


| | | | |
|---|---|---|---|
| ① 머리<br>head<br>헤드 | head | ② 눈<br>eye<br>아이 | eye |
| ③ 코<br>nose<br>노우즈 | nose | ④ 입<br>mouth<br>마우쓰 | mouth |

⑤ 이
tooth
투쓰

tooth

⑥ 귀
ear
이어

ear

⑦ 목
neck
넥

neck

⑧ 어깨
shoulder
숄더

shoulder

⑨ 가슴
chest
체스트

chest

⑩ 배
stomach
스터먹

stomach

⑪ 손
hand
핸드

hand

⑫ 다리
leg
레그

leg

⑬ 무릎
knee
니

knee

⑭ 발
foot
풋

foot

# 신체명 Ⅱ

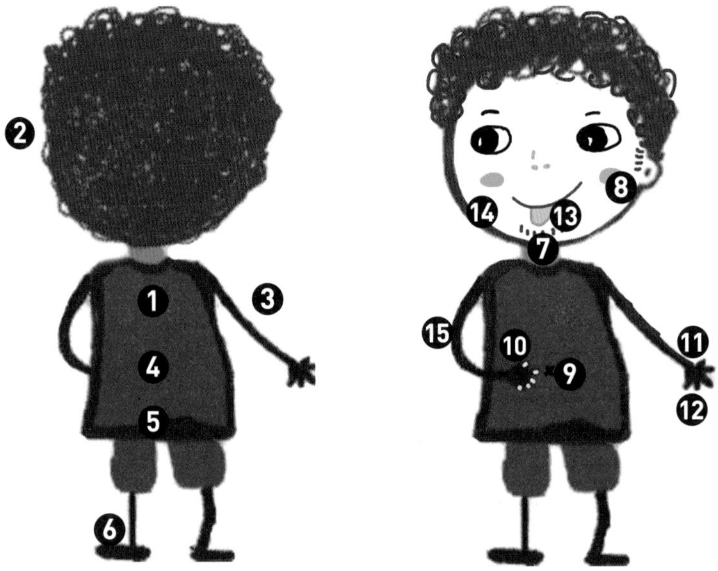

| | | | |
|---|---|---|---|
| ① 등<br>back<br>백 | back | ② 머리카락<br>hair<br>헤어 | hair |
| ③ 팔<br>arm<br>암 | arm | ④ 허리<br>waist<br>웨이스트 | waist |
| ⑤ 엉덩이<br>hip<br>힙 | hip | ⑥ 발목<br>ankle<br>앵클 | ankle |

|  |  |  |  |
|---|---|---|---|
| ⑦ 턱<br>jaw<br>줘 | jaw | 목구멍<br>throat<br>쓰롯 | throat |
| ⑧ 볼/뺨<br>cheek<br>칙 | cheek | ⑨ 배꼽<br>navel<br>네이블 | navel |
| ⑩ 손톱<br>nail<br>네일 | nail | ⑪ 손목<br>wrist<br>리스트 | wrist |
| ⑫ 손바닥<br>palm<br>팜 | palm | ⑬ 혀<br>tongue<br>텅 | tongue |
| ⑭ 피부<br>skin<br>스킨 | skin | ⑮ 팔꿈치<br>elbow<br>엘보우 | elbow |

DAY 08

# 신체명 Ⅲ

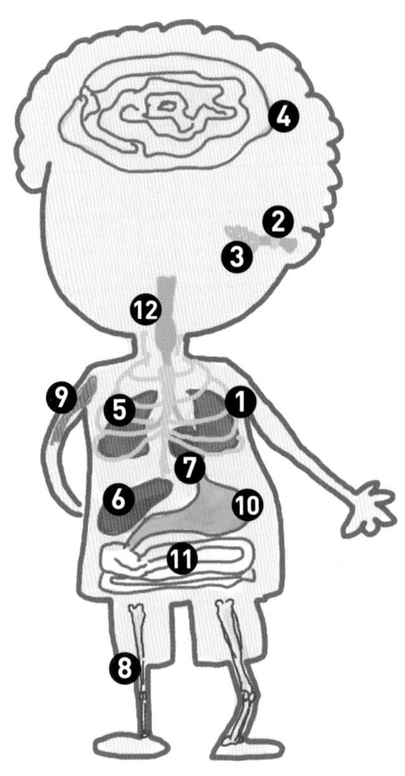


① 갈비뼈
rib
립

rib

② 고막
eardrum
이어드럼

eardrum

③ 달팽이관
cochlea
카클리어

cochlea

④ 뇌
brain
브레인

brain

⑤ 폐
lung
렁

lung

⑥ 간
liver
리버

liver

⑦ 심장
heart
할트

heart

⑧ 다리뼈
leg bone
레그 본

leg bone

⑨ 근육
muscle
머쓸

muscle

⑩ 위
stomach
스터먹

stomach

⑪ 대장
large intestine
라진테스틴

large intestine

⑫ 식도
gullet
걸럿

gullet

# 병명

|  천식<br>asthma<br>애즈머 | asthma |
|---|---|
|  고혈압<br>high blood pressure<br>하이 블러드 프레셔 | high blood pressure |
|  소화불량<br>indigestion<br>인디제스쳔 | indigestion |
| 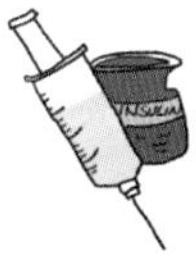 당뇨병<br>diabetes<br>다이아비디스 | diabetes |
|  심장병<br>heart disease<br>할트 디지스 | heart disease |
|  맹장염<br>appendicitis<br>어펜디사이디스 | appendicitis |
|  위염<br>gastritis<br>게스트라이디스 | gastritis |
|  배탈<br>stomachache<br>스터먹에익 | stomachache |

| | | |
|---|---|---|
|  | 감기<br>cold<br>코울드 | cold |
|  | 설사<br>diarrhea<br>다이어리어 | diarrhea |
|  | 식중독<br>food poisoning<br>푸드 포이즈닝 | food poisoning |
|  | 치통<br>toothache<br>투쎄익 | toothache |
|  | 고열<br>high fever<br>하이 피버 | high fever |
|  | 골절<br>fracture<br>프랙처 | fracture |
|  | 두통<br>headache<br>헤데익 | headache |
|  | 암<br>cancer<br>캔써 | cancer |

DAY 10

# 약명 / 생리현상

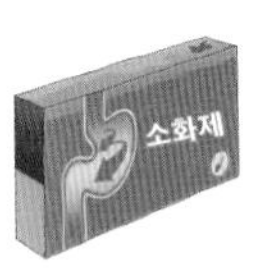


**소화제**
digestive medicine
다이제스티브 메디슨

digestive medicine

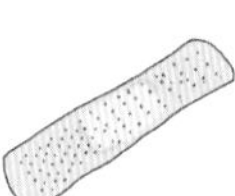

**반창고**
adhesive bandage
앳히씨브 밴디쥐

adhesive bandage

**수면제**
sleeping pill
슬리핑 필

sleeping pill

**진통제**
pain reliever / analgesic
페인 릴리버 / 애널쥐직

pain reliever / analgesic

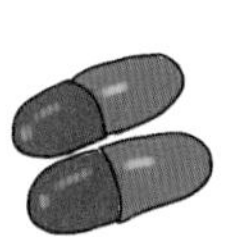

**해열제**
fever reducer / antipyretic
피버 리듀써 / 안티페이레틱

fever reducer / antipyretic

**멀미약**
motion sickness reliever
모션 씩니스 릴리버

motion sickness reliever

**기침약**
cough medicine
콥 메디슨

cough medicine

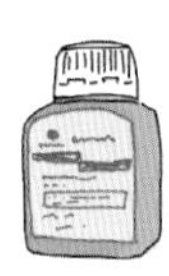

**소독약**
antiseptic
앤티셉틱

antiseptic

| | |
|---|---|
|  트림<br>burp<br>벌프 | burp |
|  재채기<br>sneeze<br>스니즈 | sneeze |
|  딸꾹질<br>hiccup<br>히껍 | hiccup |
|  하품<br>yawning<br>야닝 | yawning |
|  눈물<br>tear<br>티어 | tear |
|  대변<br>feces<br>피씨즈 | feces |
|  방귀<br>fart<br>파트 | fart |
|  소변<br>urine<br>유런 | urine |

## 연습문제A

그림을 보고 번호에 해당되는 신체부위를 영어로 써 보세요.

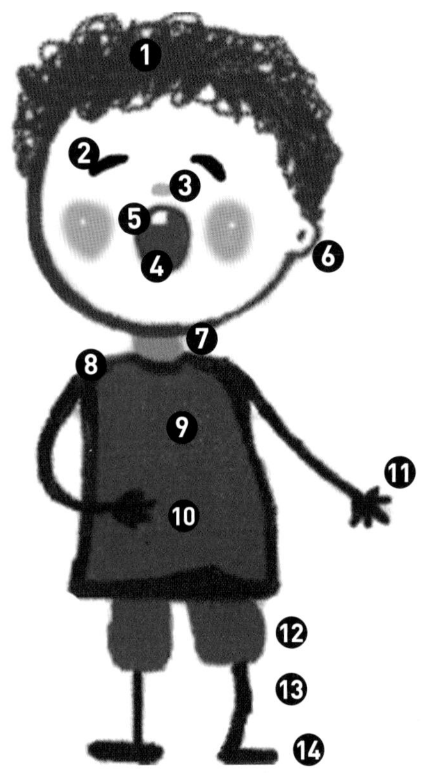


| | | | |
|---|---|---|---|
| 1. 머리 | ________ | 2. 눈 | ________ |
| 3. 코 | ________ | 4. 입 | ________ |
| 5. 이 | ________ | 6. 귀 | ________ |
| 7. 목 | ________ | 8. 어깨 | ________ |
| 9. 가슴 | ________ | 10. 배 | ________ |
| 11. 손 | ________ | 12. 다리 | ________ |
| 13. 무릎 | ________ | 14. 발 | ________ |

답 1. head 2. eye 3. nose 4.mouth 5. tooth 6. ear 7. neck 8. shoulder 9. chest 10. stomach 11. hand 12. leg 13. knee 14. foot

## 연습문제B

몸이 아파서 병원에 갔습니다. 우리말에 맞게 아픈 증상을 말하는 빈칸을 채워보세요.

1 저는 머리가 너무 아파요.

I have a ____________________.

2 저는 배탈이 났어요.

I have a ____________________.

3 저는 이가 아파요.

I have a ____________________.

4 저는 감기에 걸렸어요.

I caught a ____________________.

답 1. headache 2. stomachache 3. toothache 4. cold

# DAY 11 감정

흥분한
excited
익싸이디드

재미있는
funny
퍼니

funny

행복한
happy
해피

happy

즐거운
pleasant
플리즌트

pleasant

기쁜
glad
글래드

glad

자랑스러운
proud
프라우드

proud

감격한
deeply moved
딥플리 뭅드

deeply moved

부끄러운
ashamed
어쉐임드

ashamed

난처한
embarrassed
임베러스드

외로운
lonely
론니

화난
angry
앵그리

피곤한
tired
타이어드

지루한
bored
볼드

슬픈
sad
새드

놀란
surprised
서프라이즈드

질투하는
jealous
젤러스

DAY 12

# 칭찬 / 축하

| 멋져요<br>Great!<br>그레잇 | Great! |
|---|---|
| 훌륭해요<br>Excellent!<br>엑썰런트 | Excellent! |
| 굉장해요<br>Awesome!<br>어썸 | Awesome! |
| 대단해요<br>Wonderful!<br>원더풀 | Wonderful! |
| 귀여워요<br>Cute!<br>큐트 | Cute! |
| 예뻐요<br>Pretty!<br>프리디 | Pretty! |
| 아름다워요<br>Beautiful!<br>뷰리풀 | Beautiful! |
| 최고예요<br>Best!<br>베스트 | Best! |

| | | |
|---|---|---|
|  | 참 잘했어요<br>Good job!<br>굿 잡 | Good job! |
|  | 생일 축하합니다<br>Happy birthday.<br>해피 벌쓰데이 | Happy birthday. |
|  | 명절 잘 보내세요<br>Have a good holiday.<br>해버 굿 할러데이 | Have a good holiday. |
|  | 새해 복 많이 받으세요<br>Happy New Year.<br>해피 뉴 이어 | Happy New Year. |
|  | 즐거운 성탄절 되세요<br>Merry Christmas.<br>메리 크리스마스 | Merry Christmas. |

DAY 13

# 행동 I

| 세수하다<br>wash one's face<br>와쉬 원스 페이스 | wash one's face |
| --- | --- |
| 청소하다<br>clean<br>클린 | clean |
| 자다<br>sleep<br>슬립 | sleep |
| 일어나다<br>wake up<br>웨이컵 | wake up |
| 빨래하다<br>wash<br>와쉬 | wash |
| 먹다<br>eat<br>잇 | eat |
| 마시다<br>drink<br>드링크 | drink |
| 요리하다<br>cook<br>쿡 | cook |

| | |
|---|---|
|  설거지하다<br>do the dishes<br>두 더 디쉬스 | do the dishes |
|  양치질하다<br>brush one's teeth<br>브러쉬 원스 티쓰 | brush one's teeth |
|  샤워하다<br>take a shower<br>테이커 샤워 | take a shower |
|  옷을 입다<br>wear<br>웨어 | wear |
|  옷을 벗다<br>take off<br>테이커프 | take off |
|  쓰레기를 버리다<br>throw away garbage<br>쓰로 어웨이 가비쥐 | throw away garbage |
|  불을 켜다<br>turn on the light<br>턴 온 더 라잇 | turn on the light |
|  불을 끄다<br>turn off the light<br>턴 오프 더 라잇 | turn off the light |

# 행동 Ⅱ

| | | |
|---|---|---|
| | 오다<br>come<br>컴 | come |
| | 가다<br>go<br>고 | go |
| | 앉다<br>sit<br>싯 | sit |
| | 서다<br>stand<br>스탠드 | stand |
| | 걷다<br>walk<br>워크 | walk |
| | 달리다<br>run<br>런 | run |
| | 놀다<br>play<br>플레이 | play |
| | 웃다<br>laugh<br>래프 | laugh |

| | | |
|---|---|---|
|  | 울다<br>cry<br>크라이 | cry |
|  | 묻다<br>ask<br>애스크 | ask |
|  | 대답하다<br>answer<br>앤써 | answer |
|  | 멈추다<br>stop<br>스탑 | stop |
|  | 움직이다<br>move<br>무브 | move |
|  | 올라가다<br>go up<br>고 업 | go up |
|  | 내려가다<br>go down<br>고 다운 | go down |
|  | 읽다<br>read<br>리드 | read |

DAY 15

# 인사

|  안녕하세요<br>How are you?<br>하와 유 | How are you? |
|---|---|
|  아침인사(안녕하세요)<br>Good morning.<br>굿 모닝 | Good morning. |
|  점심인사(안녕하세요)<br>Good afternoon.<br>굿 애프터눈 | Good afternoon. |
|  저녁인사(안녕하세요)<br>Good evening.<br>굿 이브닝 | Good evening. |
|  처음 뵙겠습니다<br>How do you do?<br>하우 두 유 두 | How do you do? |
|  만나 뵙고 싶었습니다<br>I wanted to see you.<br>아이 워니드 투 씨 유 | I wanted to see you. |
|  잘 지내셨어요<br>How have you been?<br>하우 해뷰 빈 | How have you been? |
|  만나서 반갑습니다<br>Nice to meet you.<br>나이스 투 미츄 | Nice to meet you. |

| | | |
|---|---|---|
|  | 오랜만이에요<br>It's been a long time.<br>잇츠 빈 어 롱 타임 | It's been a long time. |
|  | 안녕히 가세요<br>Good bye.<br>굿 바이 | Good bye. |
|  | 또 만나요<br>See you again.<br>씨 유 어겐 | See you again. |
|  | 안녕히 주무세요<br>Good night.<br>굿 나잇 | Good night. |

## 연습문제A

영어단어에 알맞은 뜻을 연결해 보세요.

| | |
|---|---|
| 1. surprised | ⓐ 슬픈 |
| 2. Good night. | ⓑ 만나서 반갑습니다. |
| 3. Beautiful! | ⓒ 아름다워요! |
| 4. sad | ⓓ 놀란 |
| 5. Nice to meet you. | ⓔ 행복한 |
| 6. happy | ⓕ (아침인사) 안녕하세요. |
| 7. Good morning! | ⓖ 또 만나요. |
| 8. Awesome! | ⓗ 생일 축하해요. |
| 9. tired | ⓘ 안녕히 주무세요. |
| 10. See you again. | ⓙ 자랑스러운 |
| 11. proud | ⓚ 화난 |
| 12. Cute! | ⓛ 귀여워요! |
| 13. Happy birthday. | ⓜ 멋져요! |
| 14. funny | ⓝ 재미있는 |
| 15. angry | ⓞ 피곤한 |
| 16. Good job! | ⓟ 참 잘했어요! |

답 1.ⓓ 2.ⓘ 3.ⓒ 4.ⓐ 5.ⓑ 6.ⓔ 7.ⓕ 8.ⓜ 9.ⓞ 10.ⓖ 11.ⓙ 12.ⓛ 13.ⓗ 14.ⓝ 15.ⓚ 16.ⓟ

## 연습문제B

수진이의 일기를 보고 밑줄 친 부분에 알맞은 영어 단어를 적어 보세요.

| 날짜 | 7월 22일 | 날씨 | ☀ ☁ ☂ ☃ |
|---|---|---|---|

어젯밤 9시에 자서 오늘 아침 7시에 일어났다.
( ) ( )

아침밥을 먹고 세수를 하고 양치질을 했다.
( )( )

집 밖에 나가서 친구들과 신나게 놀았다.
( )

놀다가 넘어져서 울었다. 집에 걸어와서 샤워를 했다.
( ) ( )( )

엄마가 친구들과 재미있게 놀았냐고 물어봐서 그렇다고 대답했다.
( ) ( )

답 sleep, wake up, eat, wash one's(my) face, play, cry, walk, take a shower, ask, answer

# 학교 / 도형

| | | |
|---|---|---|
| | 유치원<br>kindergarten<br>킨더가든 | kindergarten |
| | 초등학교<br>primary school<br>프라이메리 스쿨 | primary school |
| | 중학교<br>middle school<br>미들 스쿨 | middle school |
| | 고등학교<br>high school<br>하이 스쿨 | high school |
| | 대학교<br>university<br>유니버씨리 | university |
| | 정사각형<br>square<br>스퀘어 | square |
| | 삼각형<br>triangle<br>트라이앵글 | triangle |
| | 원<br>circle<br>써클 | circle |

| | | |
|---|---|---|
| | 사다리꼴<br>trapezoid<br>트레퍼저이드 | trapezoid |
| | 원추형<br>cone<br>콘 | cone |
| | 다각형<br>polygon<br>팔리간 | polygon |
| | 부채꼴<br>sector<br>쎅터 | sector |
| | 타원형<br>oval<br>오블 | oval |
| 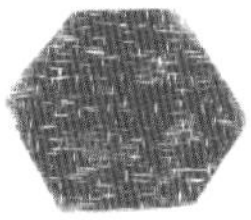 | 육각형<br>hexagon<br>핵써간 | hexagon |
| | 오각형<br>pentagon<br>펜터간 | pentagon |
| | 원기둥<br>cylinder<br>씰린더 | cylinder |

DAY 17

# 학교시설

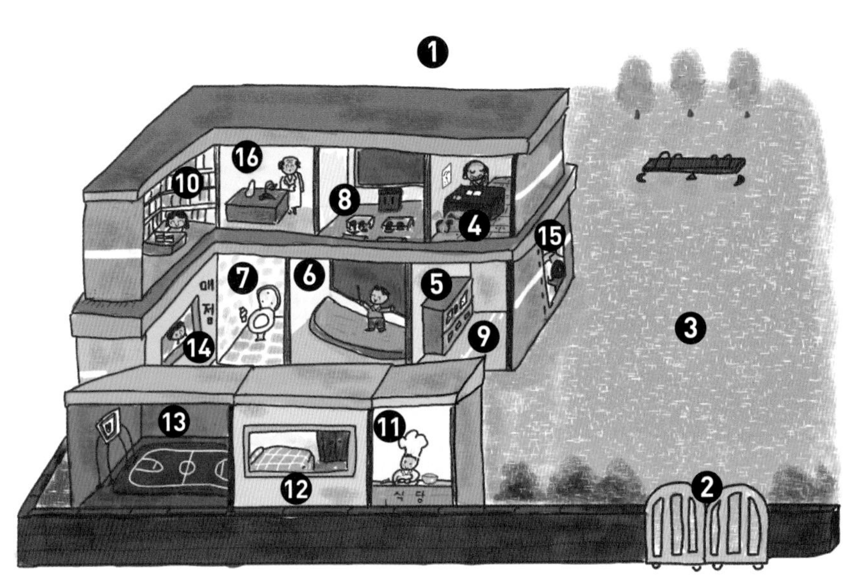


| | | | |
|---|---|---|---|
| ① 교정<br>campus<br>캠퍼스 | campus | ② 교문<br>school gate<br>스쿨 게잇 | school gate |
| ③ 운동장<br>playground<br>플레이그라운드 | playground | ④ 교장실<br>principal's office<br>프린써플소피스 | principal's office |
| ⑤ 사물함<br>locker<br>리커 | locker | ⑥ 강의실<br>lecture room<br>렉처 룸 | lecture room |

| | | | |
|---|---|---|---|
| ⑦ 화장실<br>toilet<br>토일럿 | toilet | ⑧ 교실<br>classroom<br>클래스룸 | classroom |
| ⑨ 복도<br>hallway<br>홀웨이 | hallway | ⑩ 도서관<br>library<br>라이브러리 | library |
| ⑪ 식당<br>cafeteria<br>카페테리아 | cafeteria | ⑫ 기숙사<br>dormitory<br>도미터리 | dormitory |
| ⑬ 체육관<br>gym<br>짐 | gym | ⑭ 매점<br>cafeteria<br>카페테리아 | cafeteria |
| ⑮ 교무실<br>teacher's room<br>티처스 룸 | teacher's room | ⑯ 실험실<br>laboratory<br>래브러토리 | laboratory |

DAY 18

# 교과목 및 관련 단어

| | | |
|---|---|---|
|  | 영어<br>English<br>잉글리쉬 | English |
|  | 수학<br>math<br>매쓰 | math |
|  | 경제<br>economics<br>이코노믹스 | economics |
|  | 지리<br>geography<br>쥐아그래피 | geography |
|  | 역사<br>history<br>히스토리 | history |
|  | 음악<br>music<br>뮤직 | music |
|  | 체육<br>physical education(PE)<br>피지컬 에듀케이션 | physical education(PE) |
|  | 받아쓰기<br>dictation<br>딕테이션 | dictation |

| | | |
|---|---|---|
|  | 중간고사<br>mid-term exam<br>미드텀 이그잼 | mid-term exam |
|  | 기말고사<br>final exam<br>파이널 이그잼 | final exam |
|  | 입학<br>admission<br>어드미션 | admission |
|  | 졸업<br>graduation<br>그래쥬에이션 | graduation |
|  | 숙제<br>homework<br>홈워크 | homework |
|  | 시험<br>test<br>테스트 | test |
|  | 학기<br>semester<br>씨메스터 | semester |
|  | 문학<br>literature<br>릿트러처 | literature |

DAY 19

# 학용품 I

| | | |
|---|---|---|
| | 공책(노트)<br>notebook<br>놋북 | notebook |
| | 지우개<br>eraser<br>이레이써 | eraser |
| | 볼펜<br>ball-point pen<br>볼포인트 펜 | ball-point pen |
| | 연필<br>pencil<br>펜쓸 | pencil |
| | 노트북<br>notebook<br>놋북 | notebook |
| | 책<br>book<br>북 | book |
| | 칠판<br>blackboard<br>블랙보드 | blackboard |
| | 칠판지우개<br>blackboard eraser<br>블랙보드 이레이써 | blackboard eraser |

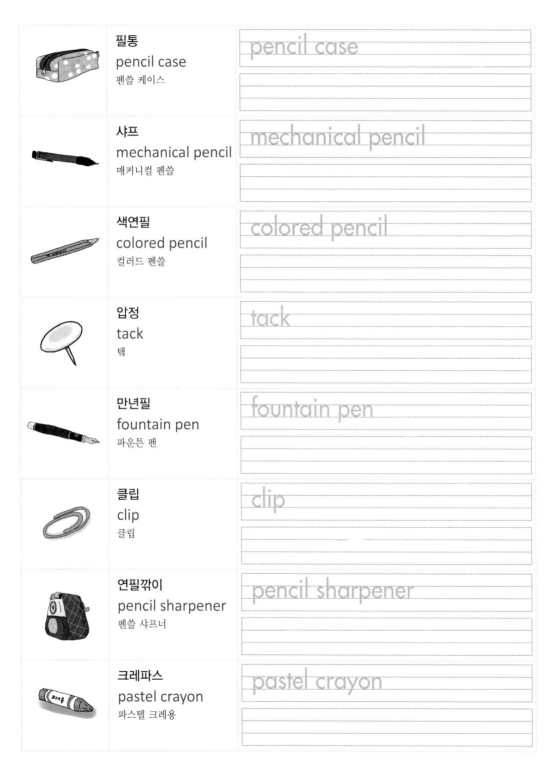

| | | |
|---|---|---|
| | 필통<br>pencil case<br>펜슬 케이스 | pencil case |
| | 샤프<br>mechanical pencil<br>매커니컬 펜슬 | mechanical pencil |
| | 색연필<br>colored pencil<br>컬러드 펜슬 | colored pencil |
| | 압정<br>tack<br>택 | tack |
| | 만년필<br>fountain pen<br>파운튼 펜 | fountain pen |
| | 클립<br>clip<br>클립 | clip |
| | 연필깎이<br>pencil sharpener<br>펜슬 샤프너 | pencil sharpener |
| | 크레파스<br>pastel crayon<br>파스텔 크레용 | pastel crayon |

DAY 20

# 학용품 Ⅱ

| | |
| --- | --- |
| 화이트<br>correction fluid<br>커렉션 플루이드 | correction fluid |
| 가위<br>scissors<br>씨저스 | scissors |
| 풀<br>glue<br>글루 | glue |
| 물감<br>paint<br>페인트 | paint |
| 잉크<br>ink<br>잉크 | ink |
| 자<br>ruler<br>룰러 | ruler |
| 스테이플러<br>stapler<br>스테플러 | stapler |
| 스케치북<br>sketchbook<br>스케치북 | sketchbook |

| | | |
|---|---|---|
| | 샤프심<br>lead<br>레드 | lead |
| | 칼<br>utility knife<br>유틸리디 나입 | utility knife |
| | 파일<br>file<br>파일 | file |
| | 매직펜<br>marker pen<br>마커 펜 | marker pen |
| | 사인펜<br>felt-tip pen<br>펠팁 펜 | felt-tip pen |
| | 형광펜<br>highlighter<br>하이라이러 | highlighter |
| | 테이프<br>tape<br>테입 | tape |
| | 콤파스<br>compass<br>컴퍼스 | compass |

## 연습문제A

그림을 보고 그림에 해당하는 알맞은 단어를 적어 보세요.

1.

2.

3.

4.

5.

6.

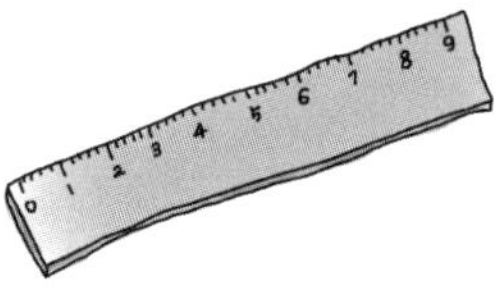

7.

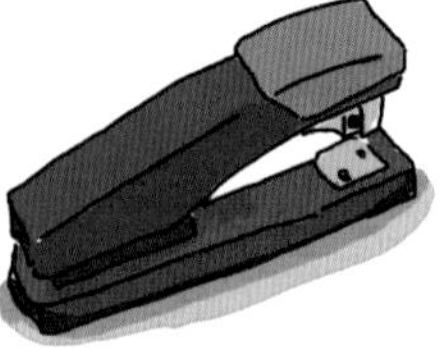

8.

답 1. square 2. triangle 3. pentagon 4. cylinder 5. eraser 6. scissors 7. ruler 8. stapler

## 연습문제B

진우의 월요일 일과 시간표를 보고 빈칸에 해당되는 영어 단어를 쓰세요.

| 월요일 | | |
|---|---|---|
| 1교시 | 수학 | |
| 2교시 | 영어 | |
| 3교시 | 음악 | |
| 점 심 | | |
| 4교시 | 체육 | |
| 5교시 | 역사 | |
| 하교 후 | 숙제 | |

답 math, English, music, PE(physical education), history, homework

DAY 21

# 부호

| | | |
|---|---|---|
| + | 더하기<br>plus<br>플러스 | plus |
| − | 빼기<br>minus<br>마이너스 | minus |
| ÷ | 나누기<br>divide<br>디바이드 | divide |
| × | 곱하기<br>times<br>타임즈 | times |
| > < | 크다/작다<br>greater/less<br>그레이러/레스 | greater/less |
| = | 같다<br>equal<br>이퀄 | equal |
| ● | 마침표<br>period<br>피리어드 | period |
| ! | 느낌표<br>exclamation mark<br>익스클러메이션 마크 | exclamation mark |

| | | |
|---|---|---|
| ? | 물음표<br>question mark<br>퀘스천 마크 | question mark |
| - | 하이픈<br>hyphen<br>하이픈 | hyphen |
| : | 콜론<br>colon<br>콜런 | colon |
| ; | 세미콜론<br>semicolon<br>쎄미콜런 | semicolon |
| " " | 따옴표<br>quotation marks<br>쿼테이션 막스 | quotation marks |
| ... | 생략기호<br>ellipsis<br>일립시즈 | ellipsis |
| @ | at/골뱅이<br>at<br>앳 | at |
| √ | 루트<br>square root<br>스퀘어 루트 | square root |

# 숫자 I

| 영<br>zero<br>지로우 | zero |
|---|---|
| 하나<br>one<br>원 | one |
| 둘<br>two<br>투 | two |
| 셋<br>three<br>쓰리 | three |
| 넷<br>four<br>포 | four |
| 다섯<br>five<br>파이브 | five |
| 여섯<br>six<br>씩스 | six |
| 일곱<br>seven<br>쎄븐 | seven |

| |  |  |
| --- | --- | --- |
| | 여덟<br>eight<br>에잇 | eight |
| | 아홉<br>nine<br>나인 | nine |
| | 열<br>ten<br>텐 | ten |
| 20 | 이십<br>twenty<br>투웬티 | twenty |
| 30 | 삼십<br>thirty<br>써리 | thirty |
| 40 | 사십<br>forty<br>포리 | forty |
| 50 | 오십<br>fifty<br>핍티 | fifty |
| 60 | 육십<br>sixty<br>씩스티 | sixty |

# 23 숫자 Ⅱ / 요일

| | | |
|---|---|---|
| 70 | 칠십<br>seventy<br>쎄븐디 | seventy |
| 80 | 팔십<br>eighty<br>에이리 | eighty |
| 90 | 구십<br>ninety<br>나인디 | ninety |
| 100 | 백<br>hundred<br>헌드레드 | hundred |
| 1,000 | 천<br>thousand<br>싸우전드 | thousand |
| 10,000 | 만<br>ten thousand<br>텐 싸우전드 | ten thousand |
| 1,000,000 | 백만<br>million<br>밀리언 | million |
| 100,000,000 | 억<br>hundred million<br>헌드레드 밀리언 | hundred million |

| | | |
|---|---|---|
| 1,000,000<br>000,000 | 조<br>trillion<br>트릴리언 | trillion |
|  | 월요일<br>Monday<br>먼데이 | Monday |
|  | 화요일<br>Tuesday<br>투스데이 | Tuesday |
|  | 수요일<br>Wednesday<br>웬즈데이 | Wednesday |
|  | 목요일<br>Thursday<br>썰스데이 | Thursday |
|  | 금요일<br>Friday<br>프라이데이 | Friday |
|  | 토요일<br>Saturday<br>쌔러데이 | Saturday |
|  | 일요일<br>Sunday<br>썬데이 | Sunday |

DAY 24

# 일 I

| | | | |
|---|---|---|---|
| 1일<br>first<br>펄스트 | first | 2일<br>second<br>쎄컨드 | second |
| 3일<br>third<br>써드 | third | 4일<br>fourth<br>폴쓰 | fourth |
| 5일<br>fifth<br>핍쓰 | fifth | 6일<br>sixth<br>씩쓰 | sixth |

| | | | |
|---|---|---|---|
| 7일<br>seventh<br>쎄븐쓰 | seventh | 8일<br>eighth<br>에잇쓰 | eighth |
| 9일<br>ninth<br>나인쓰 | ninth | 10일<br>tenth<br>텐쓰 | tenth |
| 11일<br>eleventh<br>일레븐쓰 | eleventh | 12일<br>twelfth<br>트웰프쓰 | twelfth |
| 13일<br>thirteenth<br>썰틴쓰 | thirteenth | 14일<br>fourteenth<br>폴틴쓰 | fourteenth |
| 15일<br>fifteenth<br>핍틴쓰 | fifteenth | 16일<br>sixteenth<br>씩스틴쓰 | sixteenth |

DAY 25

# 일 Ⅱ

| | | | |
|---|---|---|---|
| 17일<br>seventeenth<br>쎄븐틴쓰 | seventeenth | 18일<br>eighteenth<br>에이틴쓰 | eighteenth |
| 19일<br>nineteenth<br>나인틴쓰 | nineteenth | 20일<br>twentieth<br>트웬티쓰 | twentieth |
| 21일<br>twenty first<br>트웬티 펄스트 | twenty first | 22일<br>twenty second<br>트웬티 쎄컨드 | twenty second |

| | | | |
|---|---|---|---|
| 23일<br>twenty third<br>트웬티 써드 | twenty third | 24일<br>twenty fourth<br>트웬티 폴쓰 | twenty fourth |
| 25일<br>twenty fifth<br>트웬티 핍쓰 | twenty fifth | 26일<br>twenty sixth<br>트웬티 씩쓰 | twenty sixth |
| 27일<br>twenty seventh<br>트웬티 쎄븐쓰 | twenty seventh | 28일<br>twenty eighth<br>트웬티 에잇쓰 | twenty eighth |
| 29일<br>twenty ninth<br>트웬티 나인쓰 | twenty ninth | 30일<br>thirtieth<br>썰티쓰 | thirtieth |
| 31일<br>thirty first<br>썰티 펄스트 | thirty first | | |

Day 25 일 II

## 연습문제A

다음 숫자를 영어로 바꾸어 써 보세요.

1. 3

2. 48

3. 97

4. 186

5. 362

6. 874

7. 1,563

8. 7,768

9. 10,255

10. 1,000,067

답 1. three 2. forty eight 3. ninety seven 4. one hundred eighty six
5. three hundred sixty two 6. eight hundred seventy four
7. one thousand five hundred sixty three
8. seven thousand seven hundred sixty eight
9. ten thousand two hundred fifty five
10. one million sixty seven

다음 달력의 빈칸을 영어로 채워 보세요.

## 1월

| 일요일 | ⓐ | ⓑ | 수요일 | ⓒ | ⓓ | ⓔ |
|---|---|---|---|---|---|---|
| | 1 | 2 | 3 | 4 | ⓕ | 6 |
| ⓖ | 8 | 9 | 10 | ⓗ | 12 | ⓘ |
| 14 | ⓙ | ⓚ | 17 | 18 | 19 | ⓛ |
| ⓜ | 22 | 23 | ⓝ | 25 | 26 | 27 |
| 28 | 29 | ⓞ | 31 | | | |

답 ⓐ Monday ⓑ Tuesday ⓒ Thursday ⓓ Friday ⓔ Saturday ⓕ fifth ⓖ seventh ⓗ eleventh ⓘ thirteenth ⓙ fifteenth ⓚ sixteenth ⓛ twentieth ⓜ twenty first ⓝ twenty fourth ⓞ thirtieth

DAY 26

# 계절 / 월

| | | |
|---|---|---|
|  | 봄<br>spring<br>스프링 | spring |
|  | 여름<br>summer<br>써머 | summer |
|  | 가을<br>fall<br>펄 | fall |
|  | 겨울<br>winter<br>윈터 | winter |
|  | 1월<br>January<br>재뉴어리 | January |
|  | 2월<br>February<br>페브러리 | February |
|  | 3월<br>March<br>마취 | March |
|  | 4월<br>April<br>에이프럴 | April |

| | | |
|---|---|---|
|  | 5월<br>May<br>메이 | May |
|  | 6월<br>June<br>준 | June |
|  | 7월<br>July<br>줄라이 | July |
|  | 8월<br>August<br>어거스트 | August |
|  | 9월<br>September<br>셉템버 | September |
|  | 10월<br>October<br>악토버 | October |
|  | 11월<br>November<br>노벰버 | November |
|  | 12월<br>December<br>디쎔버 | December |

DAY 27

# 시간

| | | |
|---|---|---|
|  | 새벽<br>dawn<br>던 | dawn |
|  | 아침<br>morning<br>모닝 | morning |
|  | 오전<br>morning<br>모닝 | morning |
|  | 점심<br>lunch<br>런취 | lunch |
|  | 오후<br>afternoon<br>애프터눈 | afternoon |
|  | 저녁<br>evening<br>이브닝 | evening |
|  | 밤<br>night<br>나잇 | night |
|  | 시<br>hour<br>아우어 | hour |

| | | |
|---|---|---|
|  | 분<br>minute<br>미닛 | minute |
|  | 초<br>second<br>쎄컨드 | second |
|  5月/26 | 어제<br>yesterday<br>예스터데이 | yesterday |
|  5月/27 | 오늘<br>today<br>투데이 | today |
|  5月 28 | 내일<br>tomorrow<br>투마로우 | tomorrow |
|  5月 29 | 내일모레<br>day after tomorrow<br>데이 애프터 투마로우 | day after tomorrow |
|  | 하루<br>day<br>데이 | day |

# DAY 28 우주 환경과 오염 I

| | | |
|---|---|---|
| | 지구<br>Earth<br>얼쓰 | Earth |
| | 수성<br>Mercury<br>머큐리 | Mercury |
| | 금성<br>Venus<br>비너스 | Venus |
| | 화성<br>Mars<br>마쓰 | Mars |
| | 목성<br>Jupiter<br>쥬피터 | Jupiter |
| | 토성<br>Saturn<br>쌔턴 | Saturn |
| | 천왕성<br>Uranus<br>유러너스 | Uranus |
| | 명왕성<br>Pluto<br>플루토 | Pluto |

| | | |
|---|---|---|
| 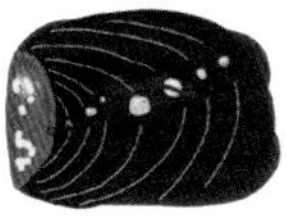 | 태양계<br>solar system<br>쏠러 씨스템 | solar system |
|  | 외계인<br>alien<br>에일리언 | alien |
| 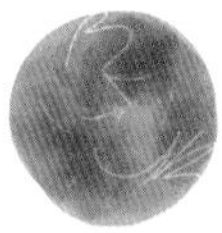 | 행성<br>planet<br>플래닛 | planet |
|  | 은하계<br>galactic system<br>걸레틱 씨스템 | galactic system |
|  | 환경<br>environment<br>인바이런먼트 | environment |
|  | 파괴<br>destruction<br>디스트럭션 | destruction |
| 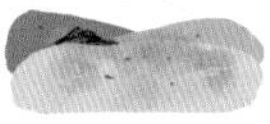 | 멸망<br>fall<br>펄 | fall |
|  | 재활용<br>recycling<br>리싸이클링 | recycling |

# DAY 29 우주 환경과 오염 Ⅱ

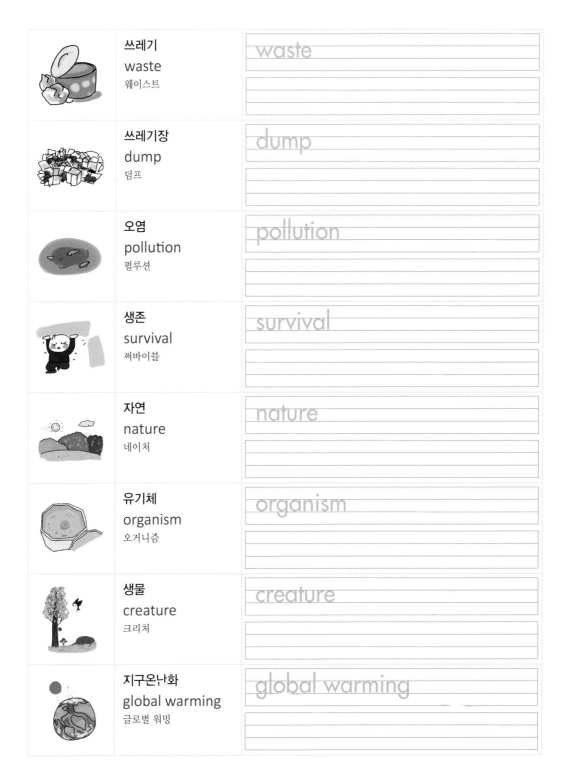

| 단어 | 쓰기 |
| --- | --- |
| 쓰레기<br>waste<br>웨이스트 | waste |
| 쓰레기장<br>dump<br>덤프 | dump |
| 오염<br>pollution<br>펄루션 | pollution |
| 생존<br>survival<br>써바이블 | survival |
| 자연<br>nature<br>네이처 | nature |
| 유기체<br>organism<br>오거니즘 | organism |
| 생물<br>creature<br>크리처 | creature |
| 지구온난화<br>global warming<br>글로벌 워밍 | global warming |

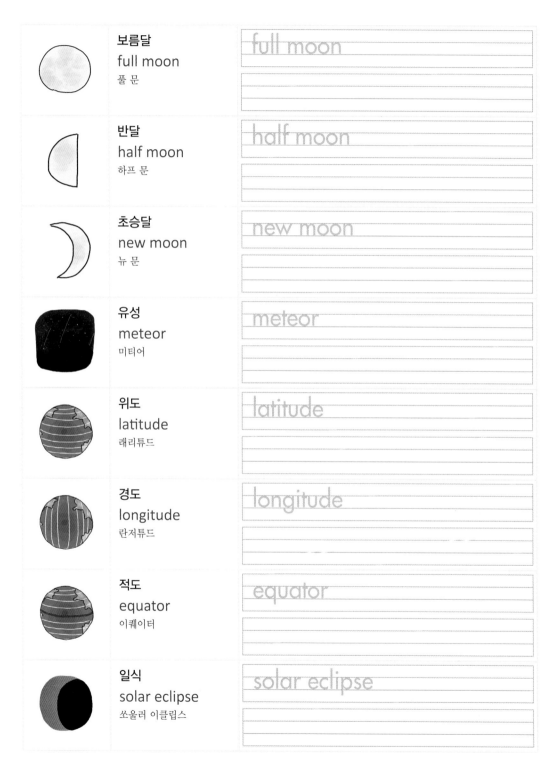

| | | | |
|---|---|---|---|
| 보름달 | full moon | 풀 문 | full moon |
| 반달 | half moon | 하프 문 | half moon |
| 초승달 | new moon | 뉴 문 | new moon |
| 유성 | meteor | 미티어 | meteor |
| 위도 | latitude | 래리튜드 | latitude |
| 경도 | longitude | 란저튜드 | longitude |
| 적도 | equator | 이퀘이터 | equator |
| 일식 | solar eclipse | 쏘울러 이클립스 | solar eclipse |

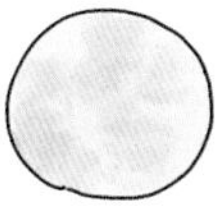

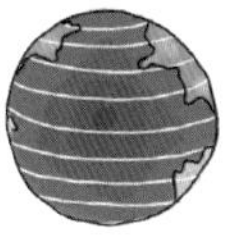

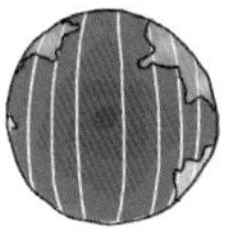

DAY 30

# 날씨 표현

| | | |
|---|---|---|
| | 맑은<br>clear<br>클리어 | clear |
| | 따뜻한<br>warm<br>웜 | warm |
| | 화창한<br>sunny<br>써니 | sunny |
| | 더운<br>hot<br>핫 | hot |
| | 흐린<br>cloudy<br>클라우디 | cloudy |
| | 안개 낀<br>foggy<br>퍼기 | foggy |
| | 습한<br>humid<br>휴미드 | humid |
| | 시원한<br>cool<br>쿨 | cool |

| | | |
|---|---|---|
|  | 쌀쌀한<br>chilly<br>칠리 | chilly |
|  | 추운<br>cold<br>코울드 | cold |
|  | 장마철<br>rainy season<br>레이니 씨즌 | rainy season |
|  | 천둥<br>thunder<br>썬더 | thunder |
| 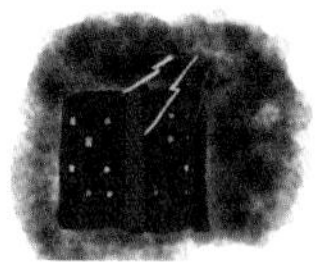 | 번개<br>lightning<br>라잇닝 | lightning |
|  | 태풍<br>typhoon<br>타이푼 | typhoon |
|  | 비가 오다<br>rain<br>레인 | rain |
|  | 눈이 내리다<br>snow<br>스노우 | snow |

# 연습문제A

영어단어에 알맞은 뜻을 연결해 보세요.

| | |
|---|---|
| 1. environment • | • ⓐ 반달 |
| 2. solar system • | • ⓑ 천둥 |
| 3. global warming • | • ⓒ 자연 |
| 4. waste • | • ⓓ 행성 |
| 5. Earth • | • ⓔ 환경 |
| 6. half moon • | • ⓕ 수성 |
| 7. Mercury • | • ⓖ 지구 온난화 |
| 8. thunder • | • ⓗ 태양계 |
| 9. planet • | • ⓘ 보름달 |
| 10. nature • | • ⓙ 쓰레기 |
| 11. typhoon • | • ⓚ 지구 |
| 12. recycling • | • ⓛ 태풍 |
| 13. Venus • | • ⓜ 비가 오다 |
| 14. full moon • | • ⓝ 눈이 오다 |
| 15. rain • | • ⓞ 재활용 |
| 16. snow • | • ⓟ 금성 |

답 1.ⓔ 2.ⓗ 3.ⓖ 4.ⓙ 5.ⓚ 6.ⓐ 7.ⓕ 8.ⓑ 9.ⓓ 10.ⓒ 11.ⓛ 12.ⓞ 13.ⓟ 14.ⓘ 15.ⓜ 16.ⓝ

## 연습문제B

빈칸에 알맞은 단어를 넣어 보세요.

**1**

A: 오늘 날씨는 어때요?

How is the weather ______________?

하우 이즈 더 웨더 투데이

B: 오늘은 화창해요.

It is ______________.

잇 이즈 써니

**2**

A: 왜 봄을 좋아해요?

Why do you like ______________?

와이 두 유 라익 스프링

B: 따뜻하니까요.

Because it is ______________.

비커즈 잇 이즈 웜

**3**

A: 12월은 춥네요.

It is ___________ in ______________.

잇 이즈 콜드 인 디쎔버

B: 감기 조심하세요.

Be careful not to catch a cold.

비 케어풀 낫 투 캐치 어 콜드

**4**

A: 명왕성이 태양계에서 소멸된 게 몇 년도인가요?

When did ____________ disappear from the solar system?

웬 디드 플루토 디써피어 프럼 더 쏘울러 씨스템

B: 2006년도요.

In 2006.

인 투싸우전씩스

답 1. today, sunny 2. spring, warm 3. cold, December 4. Pluto

DAY 31

# 날씨 관련

| | | |
|---|---|---|
|  | 해<br>sun<br>썬 | sun |
|  | 구름<br>cloud<br>클라우드 | cloud |
|  | 비<br>rain<br>레인 | rain |
| 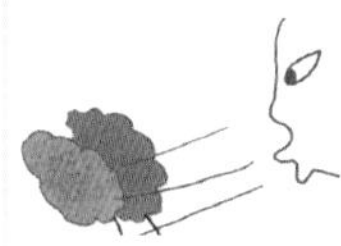 | 바람<br>wind<br>윈드 | wind |
|  | 눈<br>snow<br>스노우 | snow |
|  | 고드름<br>icicle<br>아이씨클 | icicle |
|  | 별<br>star<br>스타 | star |
|  | 달<br>moon<br>문 | moon |

**우주**
space
스페이스

**우박**
hail
헤일

**홍수**
flood
플러드

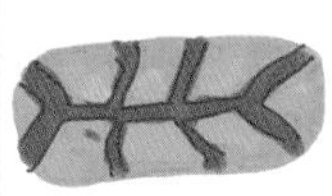

**가뭄**
drought
드라웃

**지진**
earthquake
얼쓰퀘익

**자외선**
ultraviolet rays
울트라바이얼럿 레이즈

**열대야**
tropical night
트로피컬 나잇

**오존층**
ozone layer
오우존 레이어

space
hail
flood
drought
earthquake
ultraviolet rays
tropical night
ozone layer

DAY 32 

# 포유류 I

| | | |
|---|---|---|
| | 사슴<br>deer<br>디어 | deer |
| | 고양이<br>cat<br>캣 | cat |
| | 팬더(판다)<br>panda<br>팬다 | panda |
| | 사자<br>lion<br>라이언 | lion |
| | 호랑이<br>tiger<br>타이거 | tiger |
| | 기린<br>giraffe<br>쥐래프 | giraffe |
| | 곰<br>bear<br>베어 | bear |
| | 다람쥐<br>squirrel<br>스퀴럴 | squirrel |

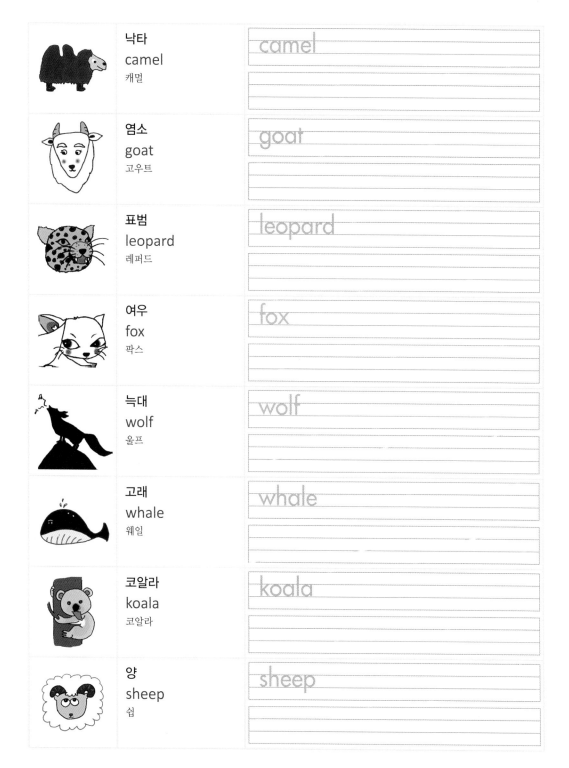


| | | |
|---|---|---|
| | 낙타<br>camel<br>캐멀 | camel |
| | 염소<br>goat<br>고우트 | goat |
| | 표범<br>leopard<br>레퍼드 | leopard |
| | 여우<br>fox<br>팍스 | fox |
| | 늑대<br>wolf<br>울프 | wolf |
| | 고래<br>whale<br>웨일 | whale |
| | 코알라<br>koala<br>코알라 | koala |
| | 양<br>sheep<br>쉽 | sheep |

# 포유류 Ⅱ

| 코끼리<br>elephant<br>엘리펀트 | elephant |
| --- | --- |
| 돼지<br>pig<br>피그 | pig |
| 말<br>horse<br>홀스 | horse |
| 원숭이<br>monkey<br>멍키 | monkey |
| 하마<br>hippo<br>히뽀 | hippo |
| 얼룩말<br>zebra<br>지브러 | zebra |
| 북극곰<br>polar bear<br>포울러 베어 | polar bear |
| 바다표범<br>seal<br>씰 | seal |

| | | |
|---|---|---|
|  | 두더지<br>mole<br>모울 | mole |
|  | 개<br>dog<br>도그 | dog |
|  | 코뿔소<br>rhinoceros<br>라이나써러스 | rhinoceros |
|  | 쥐<br>mouse<br>마우스 | mouse |
|  | 소<br>cow<br>카우 | cow |
|  | 토끼<br>rabbit<br>래빗 | rabbit |
|  | 캥거루<br>kangaroo<br>캥거루 | kangaroo |
|  | 박쥐<br>bat<br>뱃 | bat |

DAY 34

# 곤충 / 거미류

| | | |
|---|---|---|
| | 모기<br>mosquito<br>머스끼토우 | mosquito |
| | 파리<br>fly<br>플라이 | fly |
| | 벌<br>bee<br>비 | bee |
| | 잠자리<br>dragonfly<br>드래건플라이 | dragonfly |
| | 거미<br>spider<br>스파이더 | spider |
| | 매미<br>cicada<br>씨캐이더 | cicada |
| | 바퀴벌레<br>cockroach<br>칵크로취 | cockroach |
| | 귀뚜라미<br>cricket<br>크리킷 | cricket |

| | | |
|---|---|---|
|  | 풍뎅이<br>chafer<br>체이퍼 | chafer |
|  | 무당벌레<br>ladybird<br>레이디버드 | ladybird |
| 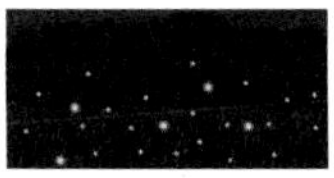 | 반딧불이<br>firefly<br>파이어플라이 | firefly |
|  | 메뚜기<br>grasshopper<br>그래스하퍼 | grasshopper |
|  | 개미<br>ant<br>앤트 | ant |
|  | 사마귀<br>mantis<br>맨티스 | mantis |
|  | 나비<br>butterfly<br>버러플라이 | butterfly |
| 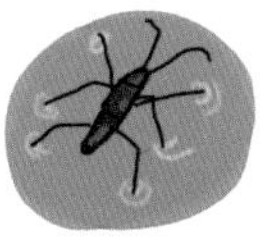 | 소금쟁이<br>pond skater<br>판 스케이터 | pond skater |

DAY 35

# 조류

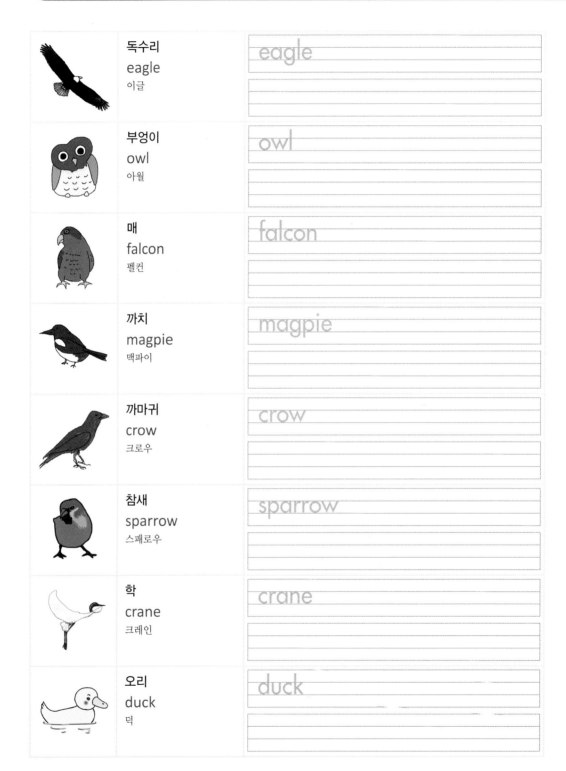

| 단어 | 쓰기 |
|---|---|
| 독수리<br>eagle<br>이글 | eagle |
| 부엉이<br>owl<br>아월 | owl |
| 매<br>falcon<br>펠컨 | falcon |
| 까치<br>magpie<br>맥파이 | magpie |
| 까마귀<br>crow<br>크로우 | crow |
| 참새<br>sparrow<br>스패로우 | sparrow |
| 학<br>crane<br>크레인 | crane |
| 오리<br>duck<br>덕 | duck |

펭귄
penguin
펭귄

penguin

제비
swallow
스왈로우

swallow

닭
chicken
취킨

chicken

공작
peacock
피콕

peacock

앵무새
parrot
페럿

parrot

기러기
wild goose
와일구스

wild goose

거위
goose
구스

goose

비둘기
dove
도브

dove

## 연습문제A

영어단어에 알맞은 뜻을 연결해 보세요.

| | |
|---|---|
| 1. ant • | • ⓐ 오리 |
| 2. owl • | • ⓑ 개미 |
| 3. duck • | • ⓒ 독수리 |
| 4. butterfly • | • ⓓ 거위 |
| 5. swallow • | • ⓔ 잠자리 |
| 6. eagle • | • ⓕ 부엉이 |
| 7. bee • | • ⓖ 벌 |
| 8. sparrow • | • ⓗ 비둘기 |
| 9. goose • | • ⓘ 나비 |
| 10. spider • | • ⓙ 거미 |
| 11. parrot • | • ⓚ 메뚜기 |
| 12. grasshopper • | • ⓛ 참새 |
| 13. dragonfly • | • ⓜ 사마귀 |
| 14. dove • | • ⓝ 모기 |
| 15. mosquito • | • ⓞ 제비 |
| 16. mantis • | • ⓟ 앵무새 |

답 1.ⓑ 2.ⓕ 3.ⓐ 4.ⓘ 5.ⓞ 6.ⓒ 7.ⓖ 8.ⓛ 9.ⓓ 10.ⓙ 11.ⓟ 12.ⓚ 13.ⓔ 14.ⓗ 15.ⓝ 16.ⓜ

## 연습문제 B

윤지가 동물원에 갔어요. 그림을 보고 동물원에서 본 동물 이름을 영어로 적어 보세요.

답 1. giraffe 2. elephant 3. lion 4. deer 5. tiger 6. bear

# 파충류 / 양서류 어류 / 연체동물 / 갑각류

| 한국어 | 영어 | 발음 | 쓰기 |
|---|---|---|---|
| 도마뱀 | lizard | 리저드 | lizard |
| 두꺼비 | toad | 토우드 | toad |
| 올챙이 | tadpole | 태드포울 | tadpole |
| 도롱뇽 | salamander | 샐러맨더 | salamander |
| 개구리 | frog | 프러그 | frog |
| 악어 | crocodile | 크라커다일 | crocodile |
| 거북이 | turtle | 터틀 | turtle |
| 뱀 | snake | 스네익 | snake |

| 우리말 | 영어 | 발음 | 따라 쓰기 |
|---|---|---|---|
| 연어 | salmon | 쌔먼 | salmon |
| 문어 | octopus | 악터퍼스 | octopus |
| 오징어 | squid | 스퀴드 | squid |
| 게 | crab | 크랩 | crab |
| 새우 | shrimp | 쉬림프 | shrimp |
| 가재 | crawfish | 크라피쉬 | crawfish |
| 상어 | shark | 샤크 | shark |
| 조개 | shellfish | 쉘피쉬 | shellfish |

# DAY 37 꽃

| | | |
|---|---|---|
|  | 무궁화<br>rose of Sharon<br>로우즈 업 쉐론 | rose of Sharon |
|  | 코스모스<br>cosmos<br>카스머스 | cosmos |
|  | 수선화<br>daffodil<br>대퍼딜 | daffodil |
|  | 장미<br>rose<br>로우즈 | rose |
|  | 데이지<br>daisy<br>데이지 | daisy |
|  | 아이리스<br>iris<br>아이리스 | iris |
|  | 동백꽃<br>camellia<br>커밀리어 | camellia |
|  | 벚꽃<br>cherry blossom<br>체리 블러썸 | cherry blossom |

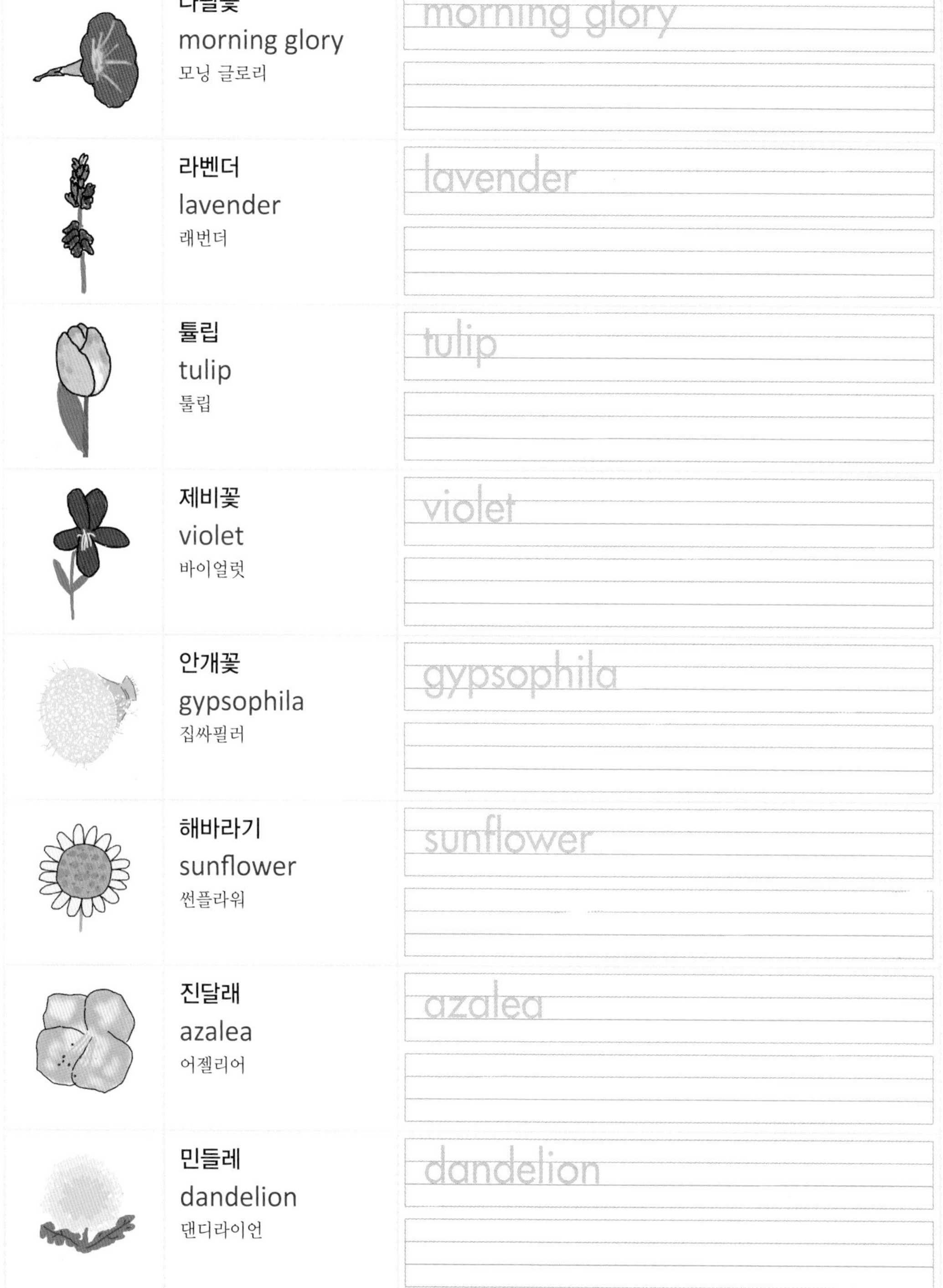

| | | |
|---|---|---|
| | 나팔꽃<br>morning glory<br>모닝 글로리 | morning glory |
| | 라벤더<br>lavender<br>래번더 | lavender |
| | 튤립<br>tulip<br>튤립 | tulip |
| | 제비꽃<br>violet<br>바이얼럿 | violet |
| | 안개꽃<br>gypsophila<br>집싸필러 | gypsophila |
| | 해바라기<br>sunflower<br>썬플라워 | sunflower |
| | 진달래<br>azalea<br>어젤리어 | azalea |
| | 민들레<br>dandelion<br>댄디라이언 | dandelion |

# 풀 / 야생화 / 나무

캐모마일
chamomile
캐머밀

chamomile

클로버
clover
클로버

clover

강아지풀
foxtail
팍스테일

foxtail

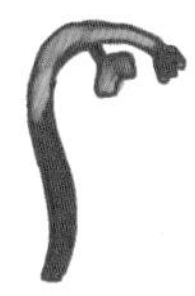

고사리
bracken
브래컨

bracken

잡초
weeds
위즈

weeds

억새풀
silvergrass
실버그래스

silvergrass

소나무
pine
파인

pine

메타세과이아
metasequoia
메터시콰이어

metasequoia

감나무
persimmon tree
퍼씨먼 트리

사과나무
apple tree
애플 트리

apple tree

석류나무
pomegranate tree
파머그래닛 트리

pomegranate tree

밤나무
chestnut tree
체스트넛 트리

chestnut tree

은행나무
ginkgo
깅코우

ginkgo

배나무
pear tree
페어 트리

pear tree

양귀비꽃
poppy
파삐

poppy

# DAY 39 집의 부속물

| | | | |
|---|---|---|---|
| ① 대문<br>gate<br>게잇 | gate | ② 담<br>wall<br>월 | wall |
| ③ 정원<br>garden<br>가든 | garden | ④ 우편함<br>mailbox<br>메일박스 | mailbox |
| ⑤ 차고<br>garage<br>거라쥐 | garage | ⑥ 진입로<br>driveway<br>드라이브웨이 | driveway |

| | | | |
|---|---|---|---|
| ⑦ 굴뚝<br>chimney<br>침니 | chimney | ⑧ 지붕<br>roof<br>루프 | roof |
| ⑨ 계단<br>stairs<br>스테얼스 | stairs | ⑩ 벽<br>wall<br>월 | wall |
| ⑪ 테라스<br>terrace<br>테러스 | terrace | ⑫ 창고<br>shed<br>쉐드 | shed |
| ⑬ 현관<br>entrance<br>엔트런스 | entrance | ⑭ 지하실<br>basement<br>베이스먼트 | basement |
| ⑮ 위층<br>upstairs<br>업스테얼스 | upstairs | ⑯ 아래층<br>downstairs<br>다운스테얼스 | downstairs |

DAY 40

# 거실용품

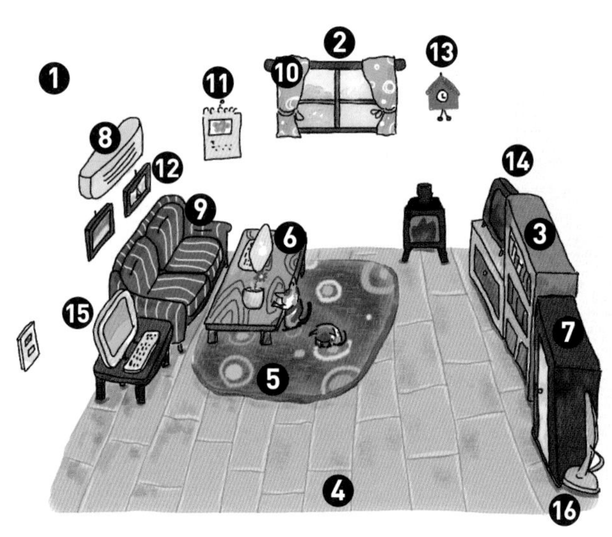

| | | | |
|---|---|---|---|
| ① 거실<br>living room<br>리빙 룸 | living room | ② 창문<br>window<br>윈도우 | window |
| ③ 책장<br>bookcase<br>북케이스 | bookcase | ④ 마루<br>floor<br>플로워 | floor |
| ⑤ 카펫<br>carpet<br>카핏 | carpet | ⑥ 테이블<br>table<br>테이블 | table |

⑦ 장식장
cabinet
캐비닛

cabinet

⑧ 에어컨
air conditioner
에어 컨디셔너

air conditioner

⑨ 소파
sofa
소우파

sofa

⑩ 커튼
curtain
커튼

curtain

⑪ 달력
calendar
캘린더

calendar

⑫ 액자
frame
프레임

frame

⑬ 시계
clock
클락

clock

⑭ 텔레비전
television
텔리비젼

television

⑮ 컴퓨터
computer
컴퓨러

computer

⑯ 진공청소기
vacuum cleaner
배큠 클리너

vacuum cleaner

## 연습문제A

영어단어에 알맞은 뜻을 연결해 보세요.

| | |
|---|---|
| 1. turtle ● | ● ⓐ 클로버 |
| 2. clover ● | ● ⓑ 상어 |
| 3. shark ● | ● ⓒ 해바라기 |
| 4. persimmon tree ● | ● ⓓ 도마뱀 |
| 5. crab ● | ● ⓔ 거북이 |
| 6. sunflower ● | ● ⓕ 장미 |
| 7. shrimp ● | ● ⓖ 소나무 |
| 8. ginkgo ● | ● ⓗ 게 |
| 9. lizard ● | ● ⓘ 감나무 |
| 10. rose ● | ● ⓙ 새우 |
| 11. snake ● | ● ⓚ 진달래 |
| 12. pine ● | ● ⓛ 뱀 |
| 13. salmon ● | ● ⓜ 은행나무 |
| 14. frog ● | ● ⓝ 벚꽃 |
| 15. azalea ● | ● ⓞ 연어 |
| 16. cherry blossom ● | ● ⓟ 개구리 |

답 1.ⓔ 2.ⓐ 3.ⓑ 4.ⓘ 5.ⓗ 6.ⓒ 7.ⓙ 8.ⓜ 9.ⓓ 10.ⓕ 11.ⓛ 12.ⓖ 13.ⓞ 14.ⓟ 15.ⓚ 16.ⓝ

## 연습문제B

지민이가 거실에서 한 일입니다. 밑줄 친 말에 해당하는 영어를 적어 보세요.

**1** 창문을 열고 환기를 시켰어요.

______________________

**2** 책장에 책을 꽂았어요.

______________________

**3** 진공청소기로 마루를 청소했어요.

__________ __________, __________

**4** 달력을 한 장 넘겼어요.

______________________

답 1. window 2. bookcase 3. vacuum cleaner, floor 4. calendar

# 41 침실용품

| | | | |
|---|---|---|---|
| ① 침대<br>bed<br>베드 | bed | ② 자명종/알람시계<br>alarm<br>얼람 | alarm |
| ③ 매트리스<br>mattress<br>매트리스 | mattress | ④ 침대시트<br>bed sheet<br>베드 쉿 | bed sheet |
| ⑤ 슬리퍼<br>slippers<br>슬리퍼스 | slippers | ⑥ 이불<br>bedclothes<br>베드클로우쓰 | bedclothes |

⑦ 베개
pillow
필로우

pillow

⑧ 화장대
dressing table
드레싱 테이블

dressing table

⑨ 화장품
cosmetics
코스메릭스

cosmetics

⑩ 옷장
closet
클로짓

closet

⑪ 쿠션
cushion
쿠션

cushion

⑫ 쓰레기통
garbage can
가비쥐 캔

garbage can

⑬ 천장
ceiling
씰링

ceiling

⑭ 전등
electric light
일렉트릭 라잇

electric light

⑮ 스위치
switch
스위취

switch

⑯ 공기청정기
air purifier
에어 퓨러파이어

air purifier

DAY 42

# 주방 / 주방용품

| | | | |
|---|---|---|---|
| ① 냉장고<br>refrigerator<br>리프리져레이러 | refrigerator | ② 전자레인지<br>microwave<br>마이크로웨이브 | microwave |
| ③ 환풍기<br>ventilator<br>벤틸레이러 | ventilator | ④ 가스레인지<br>gas stove<br>개스 스토브 | gas stove |
| ⑤ 싱크대<br>sink<br>씽크 | sink | ⑥ 주방조리대<br>countertop<br>카운터탑 | countertop |
| ⑦ 오븐<br>oven<br>오븐 | oven | ⑧ 수납장<br>cabinet<br>캐비닛 | cabinet |

| | | |
|---|---|---|
| | 도마<br>cutting board<br>커팅 보드 | cutting board |
| | 프라이팬<br>frying pan<br>프라잉 팬 | frying pan |
| | 칼<br>knife<br>나이프 | knife |
| | 뒤집개<br>spatula<br>스페츌러 | spatula |
| | 국자<br>ladle<br>레이들 | ladle |
| | 냄비<br>pot<br>팟 | pot |
| | 젓가락<br>chopsticks<br>찹스틱스 | chopsticks |
| | 숟가락<br>spoon<br>스푼 | spoon |

DAY 43

# 욕실용품

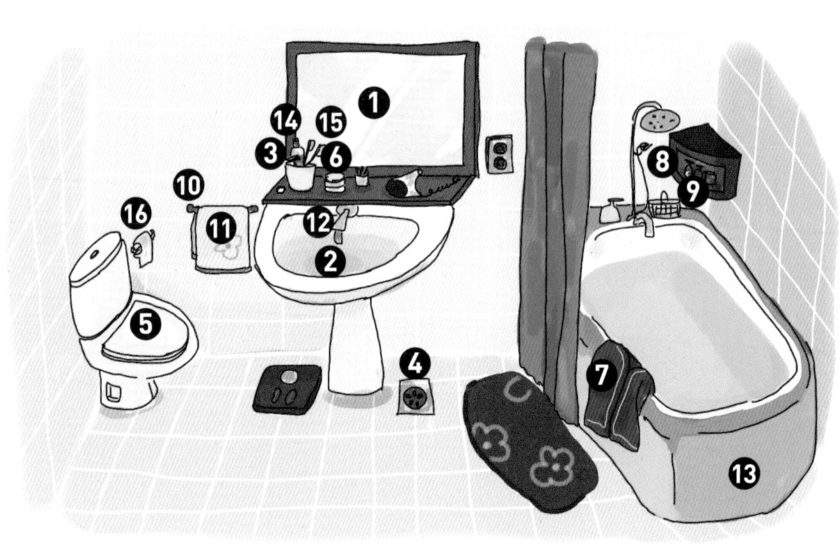

| | | | |
|---|---|---|---|
| ① 거울<br>mirror<br>미러 | mirror | ② 세면대<br>sink<br>씽크 | sink |
| ③ 면도기<br>razor /<br>(전기) shaver<br>레이저/쉐이버 | razor / shaver | ④ 배수구<br>drain<br>드레인 | drain |
| ⑤ 변기<br>toilet<br>토일럿 | toilet | ⑥ 비누<br>soap<br>쏘웁 | soap |

| | | | |
|---|---|---|---|
| ⑦ 샤워가운<br>bathrobe<br>배쓰로웁 | bathrobe | ⑧ 샴푸<br>shampoo<br>샘푸 | shampoo |
| ⑨ 린스<br>hair conditioner<br>헤어 컨디셔너 | hair conditioner | ⑩ 수건걸이<br>towel rack<br>타월 랙 | towel rack |
| ⑪ 수건<br>towel<br>타월 | towel | ⑫ 수도꼭지<br>faucet<br>퍼씻 | faucet |
| ⑬ 욕조<br>bathtub<br>배쓰텁 | bathtub | ⑭ 치약<br>toothpaste<br>투쓰페이스트 | toothpaste |
| ⑮ 칫솔<br>toothbrush<br>투쓰브러쉬 | toothbrush | ⑯ 화장지<br>toilet paper<br>토일럿 페이퍼 | toilet paper |

DAY 44

# 채소, 뿌리식물 I

| | | |
|---|---|---|
|  | 고수나물<br>coriander<br>커리앤더 | coriander |
|  | 양상추<br>(iceberg) lettuce<br>(아이스벅) 레티스 | (iceberg) lettuce |
|  | 애호박<br>zucchini<br>주키니 | zucchini |
|  | 당근<br>carrot<br>캐럿 | carrot |
|  | 피망<br>bell pepper<br>벨 페퍼 | bell pepper |
|  | 버섯<br>mushroom<br>머쉬룸 | mushroom |
| 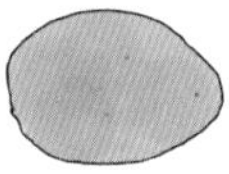 | 감자<br>potato<br>포테이도 | potato |
|  | 고추<br>chili pepper<br>칠리 페퍼 | chili pepper |

| | | |
|---|---|---|
|  | 토마토<br>tomato<br>토메이도 | tomato |
| 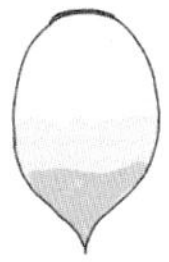 | 무<br>radish<br>래디쉬 | radish |
|  | 배추<br>napa cabbage<br>나파 캐비쥐 | napa cabbage |
|  | 마늘<br>garlic<br>갈릭 | garlic |
| 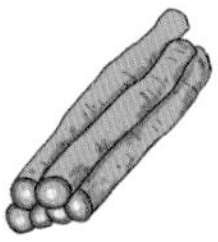 | 우엉<br>burdock<br>버닥 | burdock |
| 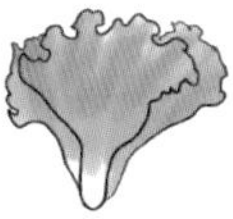 | 상추<br>(leaf) lettuce<br>(립) 레티스 | (leaf) lettuce |
|  | 시금치<br>spinach<br>스피니취 | spinach |
|  | 양배추<br>cabbage<br>캐비쥐 | cabbage |

# 채소, 뿌리식물 Ⅱ

|  |  |
|---|---|
|  양파<br>onion<br>어니언 | onion |
|  호박<br>pumpkin<br>펌킨 | pumpkin |
| 고구마<br>sweet potato<br>스윗 포테이도 | sweet potato |
| 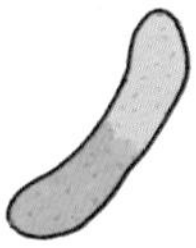 오이<br>cucumber<br>큐컴버 | cucumber |
|  파<br>green onion<br>그린 어니언 | green onion |
|  콩나물<br>bean sprouts<br>빈 스프라웃 | bean sprouts |
|  생강<br>ginger<br>진저 | ginger |
|  미나리<br>water dropwort<br>워러 드랍웟 | water dropwort |

| |  |  |  |  |
|---|---|---|---|---|
| | 옥수수 | corn | 콘 | corn |
|  | 가지 | eggplant | 에그플랜트 | eggplant |
|  | 송이버섯 | pine mushroom | 파인 머쉬룸 | pine mushroom |
| 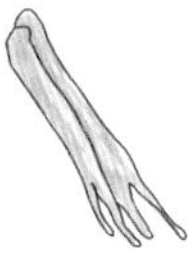 | 도라지 | balloon flower | 벌룬 플라워 | balloon flower |
|  | 깻잎 | perilla leaf | 페릴라 립 | perilla leaf |
|  | 고사리 | bracken | 브래컨 | bracken |
|  | 인삼 | ginseng | 진셍 | ginseng |
|  | 홍삼 | red ginseng | 레드 진셍 | red ginseng |

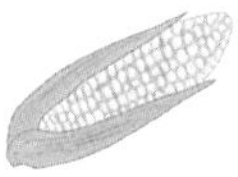

## 연습문제A

영어단어에 알맞은 뜻을 연결해 보세요.

| | |
|---|---|
| 1. onion | ⓐ 고구마 |
| 2. pumpkin | ⓑ 오이 |
| 3. carrot | ⓒ 마늘 |
| 4. sweet potato | ⓓ 콩나물 |
| 5. cucumber | ⓔ 양파 |
| 6. potato | ⓕ 감자 |
| 7. garlic | ⓖ 당근 |
| 8. bean sprouts | ⓗ 호박 |
| 9. ginger | ⓘ 피망 |
| 10. spinach | ⓙ 시금치 |
| 11. bell pepper | ⓚ 생강 |
| 12. mushroom | ⓛ 양배추 |
| 13. cabbage | ⓜ 인삼 |
| 14. radish | ⓝ 버섯 |
| 15. ginseng | ⓞ 무 |
| 16. corn | ⓟ 옥수수 |

답 1.ⓔ 2.ⓗ 3.ⓖ 4.ⓐ 5.ⓑ 6.ⓕ 7.ⓒ 8.ⓓ 9.ⓚ 10.ⓙ 11.ⓘ 12.ⓝ 13.ⓛ 14.ⓞ 15.ⓜ 16.ⓟ

## 연습문제B

모모가 침실과 주방에서 한 일들이에요.
밑줄 친 단어에 해당하는 영어 단어를
적어 보세요.

1 냉장고 문을 열어 음료수를 꺼내 마셨어요.

______________________

2 옷장에서 옷을 꺼내 입었어요.

______________________

3 베개에 씌워져 있는 커버를 갈았어요.

______________________

4 도마 위에 채소를 올려 칼로 잘게 잘랐어요.

____________ ____________, ____________

답 1. refrigerator 2. closet 3. pillow 4. cutting board, knife

DAY 46

# 과일

| | | |
|---|---|---|
| | 사과<br>apple<br>애플 | apple |
| | 배<br>pear<br>페어 | pear |
| | 참외<br>oriental melon<br>어리엔틀 멜런 | oriental melon |
| | 수박<br>watermelon<br>워러멜런 | watermelon |
| | 복숭아<br>peach<br>피취 | peach |
| | 멜론<br>melon<br>멜런 | melon |
| | 오렌지<br>orange<br>어린쥐 | orange |
| | 레몬<br>lemon<br>레먼 | lemon |

|  |  |  |  |
|---|---|---|---|
| 바나나 | banana | 버내너 | banana |
| 자두 | plum | 플럼 | plum |
| 살구 | apricot | 애프리캇 | apricot |
| 감 | persimmon | 퍼씨먼 | persimmon |
| 파인애플 | pineapple | 파인애플 | pineapple |
| 키위 | kiwi | 키위 | kiwi |
| 포도 | grape | 그레이프 | grape |
| 딸기 | strawberry | 스트로베리 | strawberry |

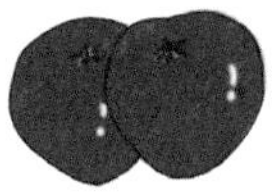

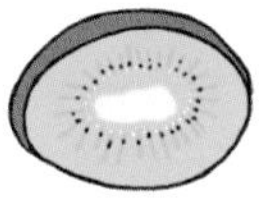

DAY 47

# 수산물, 해조류 / 육류

|  |  |
|---|---|
|  전복<br>abalone<br>애벌로니 | abalone |
|  멍게<br>sea squirt<br>씨 스쿼트 | sea squirt |
|  성게<br>sea urchin<br>씨 어친 | sea urchin |
|  해삼<br>sea cucumber<br>씨 큐컴버 | sea cucumber |
| 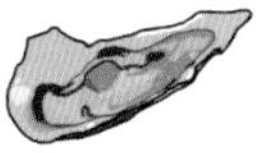 굴<br>oyster<br>오이스터 | oyster |
|  미역<br>seaweed<br>씨위드 | seaweed |
|  김<br>laver<br>라버 | laver |
|  소고기<br>beef<br>비프 | beef |

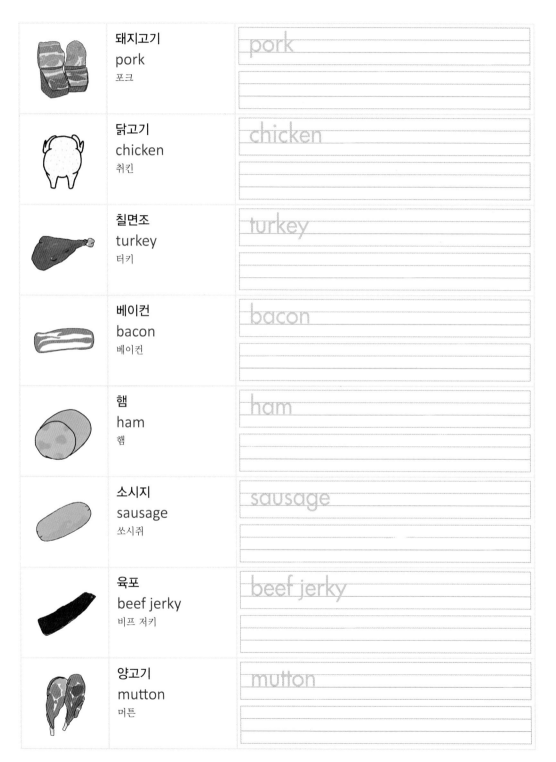


| | | |
|---|---|---|
| | 돼지고기<br>pork<br>포크 | pork |
| | 닭고기<br>chicken<br>취킨 | chicken |
| | 칠면조<br>turkey<br>터키 | turkey |
| | 베이컨<br>bacon<br>베이컨 | bacon |
| | 햄<br>ham<br>햄 | ham |
| | 소시지<br>sausage<br>쏘시쥐 | sausage |
| | 육포<br>beef jerky<br>비프 저키 | beef jerky |
| | 양고기<br>mutton<br>머튼 | mutton |

DAY 48

# 음료수

| | | |
|---|---|---|
|   | 콜라(코카콜라)<br>Coke<br>코우크 | Coke |
|   | 사이다(스프라이트)<br>Sprite<br>스프라잇 | Sprite |
|  | 커피<br>coffee<br>커피 | coffee |
|  | 핫초코<br>hot chocolate<br>핫 차컬릿 | hot chocolate |
|  | 홍차<br>black tea<br>블랙 티 | black tea |
|  | 녹차<br>green tea<br>그린 티 | green tea |
|  | 밀크버블티<br>milkbubble tea<br>밀크버블 티 | milkbubble tea |
|  | 자스민차<br>jasmine tea<br>재스민 티 | jasmine tea |

| | | |
|---|---|---|
|  | 밀크티<br>milk tea<br>밀크 티 |  milk tea |
|  | 우유<br>milk<br>밀크 |  milk |
|  | 두유<br>soybean milk<br>쏘이빈 밀크 | soybean milk |
|  | 생수<br>mineral water<br>미너럴 워러 | mineral water |
|  | 오렌지주스<br>orange juice<br>어린쥐 쥬스 | orange juice |
|  | 레모네이드<br>lemonade<br>레머네이드 | lemonade |
|  | 요구르트<br>yogurt<br>요걸 | yogurt |

# DAY 49 기타 식품 및 요리재료

| | | |
|---|---|---|
| | 치즈<br>cheese<br>취즈 | cheese |
| | 요거트<br>yogurt<br>요것 | yogurt |
| | 아이스크림<br>ice cream<br>아이스 크림 | ice cream |
| | 분유<br>powdered milk<br>파우더드 밀크 | powdered milk |
| | 버터<br>butter<br>버러 | butter |
| | 참치<br>tuna<br>튜나 | tuna |
| | 식용유<br>cooking oil<br>쿠킹 오일 | cooking oil |
| | 간장<br>soy sauce<br>쏘이 쏘스 | soy sauce |

| | | |
|---|---|---|
| 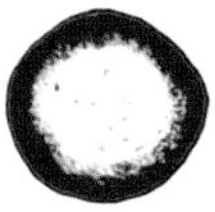 | 소금<br>salt<br>쏠트 | salt |
|  | 설탕<br>sugar<br>슈거 | sugar |
|  | 식초<br>vinegar<br>비니거 | vinegar |
|  | 참기름<br>sesame oil<br>쎄써미 오일 | sesame oil |
| 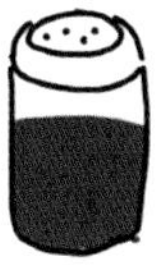 | 후추<br>pepper<br>페퍼 | pepper |
| 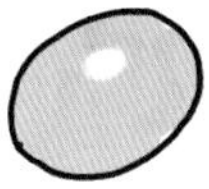 | 달걀<br>egg<br>에그 | egg |

DAY 50

# 대표요리

| | | |
|---|---|---|
|  | 햄버거<br>hamburger<br>햄버거 | hamburger |
| 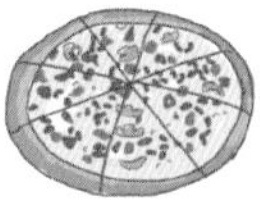 | 피자<br>pizza<br>핏짜 | pizza |
| 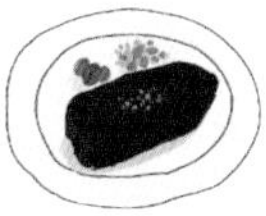 | 스테이크<br>steak<br>스테익 | steak |
| 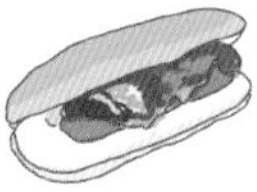 | 핫도그<br>hot dog<br>핫도그 | hot dog |
|  | 마카로니 앤 치즈<br>macaroni and cheese<br>매커로니 앤 취즈 | macaroni and cheese |
|  | 포테이토칩<br>potato chips<br>포테이도 칩스 | potato chips |
| 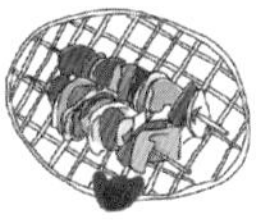 | 바비큐<br>barbecue<br>바비큐 | barbecue |
|  | 파스타<br>pasta<br>파스타 | pasta |

| | | |
|---|---|---|
|  | 바게뜨<br>baguette<br>배겟 | baguette |
|  | 타르트<br>tart<br>타르트 | tart |
|  | 샌드위치<br>sandwich<br>쌘드위취 | sandwich |
|  | 파니니<br>panini<br>파니니 | panini |
| 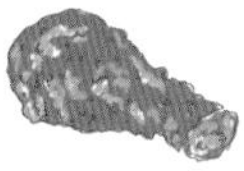 | 프라이드치킨<br>fried chicken<br>프라이드 취킨 | fried chicken |
| 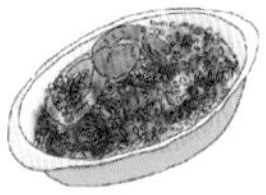 | 리조또<br>risotto<br>리조토 | risotto |
| 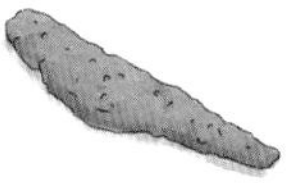 | 피시 앤 칩스<br>fish and chips<br>피쉬 앤 칩스 | fish and chips |
|  | 와플<br>waffle<br>와플 | waffle |

## 연습문제A

영어단어에 알맞은 뜻을 연결해 보세요.

| | |
|---|---|
| 1. peach • | • ⓐ 복숭아 |
| 2. watermelon • | • ⓑ 굴 |
| 3. oyster • | • ⓒ 녹차 |
| 4. green tea • | • ⓓ 배 |
| 5. grape • | • ⓔ 수박 |
| 6. chicken • | • ⓕ 참치 |
| 7. pear • | • ⓖ 포도 |
| 8. tuna • | • ⓗ 소고기 |
| 9. beef • | • ⓘ 간장 |
| 10. seaweed • | • ⓙ 닭고기 |
| 11. soy sauce • | • ⓚ 미역 |
| 12. apple • | • ⓛ 우유 |
| 13. soybean milk • | • ⓜ 두유 |
| 14. strawberry • | • ⓝ 돼지고기 |
| 15. milk • | • ⓞ 딸기 |
| 16. pork • | • ⓟ 사과 |

답 1.ⓐ 2.ⓔ 3.ⓑ 4.ⓒ 5.ⓖ 6.ⓙ 7.ⓓ 8.ⓕ 9.ⓗ 10.ⓚ 11.ⓘ 12.ⓟ 13.ⓜ 14.ⓞ 15.ⓛ 16.ⓝ

## 연습문제B

은성이가 음식점에 갔어요. 메뉴판을 보고 메뉴판에 있는 음식의 영어 이름을 써 보세요.

# MENU

피자 ---------- 20,000원

(　　　　　　　　　　)

파스타 ---------- 10,000원

(　　　　　　　　　　)

리조또 ---------- 10,000원

(　　　　　　　　　　)

핫도그 ---------- 3,000원

(　　　　　　　　　　)

햄버거 ---------- 5,000원

(　　　　　　　　　　)

샌드위치 ---------- 6,000원

(　　　　　　　　　　)

타르트 ---------- 6,000원

(　　　　　　　　　　)

답 pizza, pasta, risotto, hot dog, hamburger, sandwich, tart

# DAY 51 맛 표현

맛있는
delicious
딜리셔스

delicious

맛없는
bad
배드

bad

싱거운
bland
블랜드

bland

뜨거운
hot
핫

hot

단
sweet
스윗

sweet

짠
salty
쏠티

salty

매운
spicy
스파이씨

spicy

얼큰한
spicy
스파이씨

spicy

신
sour
싸워

쓴
bitter
비러

떫은
astringent
어스트린젼트

느끼한
greasy
그리씨

(곡식이나 견과류 등이) 고소한
nutty
너티

담백한
mild
마일드

쫄깃한
chewy
츄이

비린
fishy
피쉬

# DAY 52 의류

| |  |  |
|---|---|---|
| | 정장<br>suit<br>슛 | suit |
| | 청바지<br>jeans<br>진스 | jeans |
| | 티셔츠<br>T-shirt<br>티셔츠 | T-shirt |
| | 원피스<br>dress<br>드레스 | dress |
| | 반바지<br>shorts<br>쇼츠 | shorts |
| | 치마<br>skirt<br>스커트 | skirt |
| | 조끼<br>vest<br>베스트 | vest |
| | 남방<br>shirt<br>셔츠 | shirt |

| | | |
|---|---|---|
|  | 재킷<br>jacket<br>재킷 | jacket |
|  | 운동복<br>sportswear<br>스포츠웨어 | sportswear |
|  | 스웨터<br>sweater<br>스웨러 | sweater |
|  | 우의<br>raincoat<br>레인코웃 | raincoat |
|  | 속옷<br>underwear<br>언더웨어 | underwear |
|  | 교복<br>school uniform<br>스쿨 유니폼 | school uniform |
|  | 바지<br>pants<br>팬츠 | pants |
|  | 외투<br>overcoat<br>오버코웃 | overcoat |

DAY 53

# 신발, 양말 / 기타 액세서리

| | | |
|---|---|---|
| | 신발<br>shoes<br>슈즈 | shoes |
| | 운동화<br>sneakers<br>스니커스 | sneakers |
| | 구두<br>shoes<br>슈즈 | shoes |
| | 부츠<br>boots<br>부츠 | boots |
| | 슬리퍼<br>slippers<br>슬리퍼스 | slippers |
| | (비 올 때 신는) 장화<br>rain boots<br>레인 부츠 | rain boots |
| | 양말<br>socks<br>싹스 | socks |
| | 스타킹<br>stockings<br>스타킹스 | stockings |

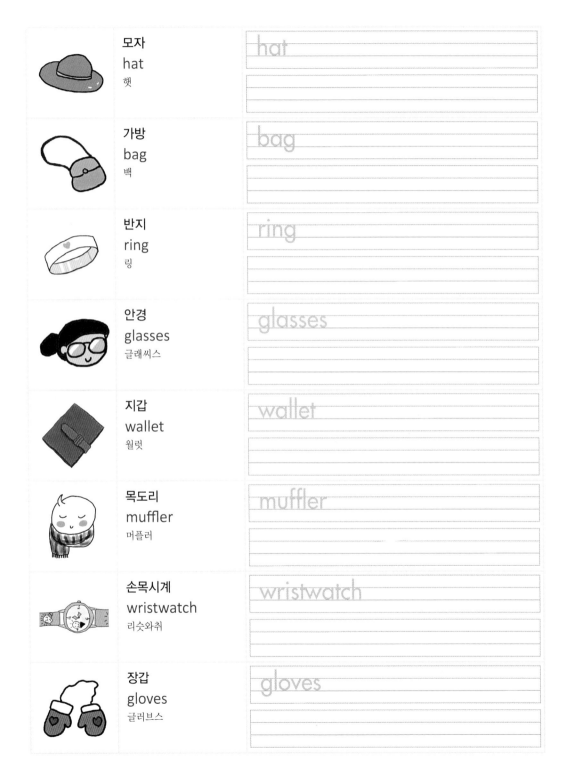


| 뜻 | 단어 | 발음 | 따라 쓰기 |
|---|---|---|---|
| 모자 | hat | 햇 | hat |
| 가방 | bag | 백 | bag |
| 반지 | ring | 링 | ring |
| 안경 | glasses | 글래씨스 | glasses |
| 지갑 | wallet | 월럿 | wallet |
| 목도리 | muffler | 머플러 | muffler |
| 손목시계 | wristwatch | 리슷와춰 | wristwatch |
| 장갑 | gloves | 글러브스 | gloves |

DAY 54 기타용품

| | | |
|---|---|---|
| | 비누<br>soap<br>쏘웁 | soap |
| | 물티슈<br>wet wipe<br>웻 와입 | wet wipe |
| | 기저귀<br>diaper<br>다이퍼 | diaper |
| | 우산<br>umbrella<br>엄브렐러 | umbrella |
| | 건전지<br>battery<br>배러리 | battery |
| | 종이컵<br>paper cup<br>페이퍼 컵 | paper cup |
| | 모기약<br>mosquito repellent<br>머스끼토우 리펠런트 | mosquito repellent |
| | 컵라면<br>cup noodles<br>컵 누들스 | cup noodles |

| | | |
|---|---|---|
|  | 면도크림<br>shaving cream<br>쉐이빙 크림 | shaving cream |
|  | 치약<br>toothpaste<br>투쓰페이스트 | toothpaste |
|  | 칫솔<br>toothbrush<br>투쓰브러쉬 | toothbrush |
|  | 손톱깎이<br>nail clippers<br>네일 클리퍼스 | nail clippers |
|  | 화장지<br>toilet paper<br>토일럿 페이퍼 | toilet paper |
| 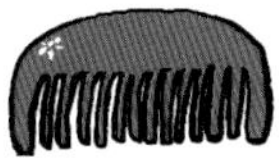 | 빗<br>comb<br>코움 | comb |
|  | 향수<br>perfume<br>퍼퓸 | perfume |
|  | 거울<br>mirror<br>미러 | mirror |

DAY 55

# 색상

| | | |
|---|---|---|
| | 빨간색<br>red<br>레드 | red |
| | 주황색<br>orange<br>어린쥐 | orange |
| | 노란색<br>yellow<br>옐로우 | yellow |
| | 초록색<br>green<br>그린 | green |
| | 파란색<br>blue<br>블루 | blue |
| | 남색<br>navy<br>네이비 | navy |
| | 보라색<br>purple<br>퍼플 | purple |
| | 상아색<br>ivory<br>아이버리 | ivory |

| | | |
|---|---|---|
| | 황토색<br>ocher<br>오우커 | ocher |
| 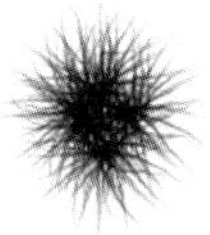 | 검은색<br>black<br>블랙 | black |
| 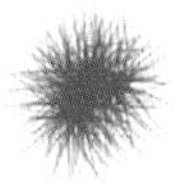 | 회색<br>gray<br>그레이 | gray |
|  | 흰색<br>white<br>와잇 | white |
|  | 갈색<br>brown<br>브라운 | brown |
| 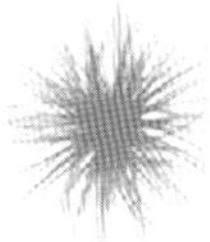 | 분홍색<br>pink<br>핑크 | pink |

## 연습문제A

그림을 보고 해당되는 영어 단어를 쓰세요.

1.

2.

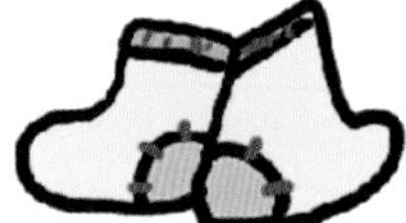

3.

4.

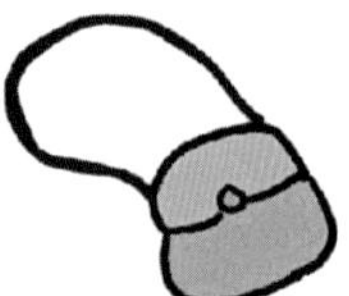

5.

6.

7.

8.

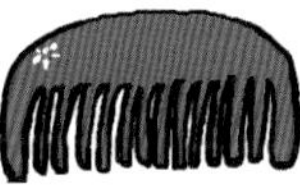

9.

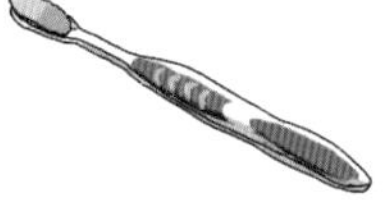

10.

답 1. skirt 2. school uniform 3. socks 4. hat 5. bag 6. glasses 7. umbrella 8. toilet paper 9. comb 10. toothbrush

## 연습문제 B

빈칸에 알맞은 단어를 넣어 보세요.

1

A: 이 와플 맛이 어때요?

How does this waffle taste?

하우 더즈 디스 와플 테이스트

B: 맛있어요!

It is ________________!

잇 이즈 딜리셔스

2

A: 도와드릴까요?

May I help you?

메이 아이 헬퓨

B: 저는 청바지를 사려고 해요.

I want to buy ______________.

아이 원투 바이 진스

3

A: 무슨 색깔을 좋아해요?

What color do you like?

왓 칼라 두 유 라익

B: 저는 빨간색을 좋아해요.

I like ____________.

아이 라익 레드

4

A: 파란색을 보면 마음이 편해져요.

__________ makes me feel better.

블루 메익스 미 필 베러

B: 저는 초록색을 보면 마음이 편해져요.

I feel better when I see ____________.

아이 필 베러 웬 아이 씨 그린

답 1. delicious 2. jeans 3. red 4. Blue, green

# 자연물 또는 인공물

| | | |
|---|---|---|
| | 강<br>river<br>리버 | river |
| | 나무<br>tree<br>트리 | tree |
| | 동굴<br>cave<br>케이브 | cave |
| | 들판<br>field<br>필드 | field |
| | 바다<br>sea<br>씨 | sea |
| | 사막<br>desert<br>데저트 | desert |
| | 산<br>mountain<br>마운튼 | mountain |
| | 섬<br>island<br>아일런드 | island |

|  |  |  |  |
|---|---|---|---|
| 삼림 | forest | 퍼리스트 | forest |
| 습지 | wetland | 웻랜드 | wetland |
| 연못 | pond | 판드 | pond |
| 폭포 | waterfall | 워러펄 | waterfall |
| 해안 | coast | 코우스트 | coast |
| 협곡 | canyon | 캐년 | canyon |
| 호수 | lake | 레익 | lake |
| 목장 | farm | 팜 | farm |

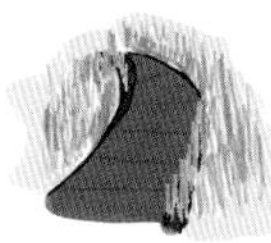

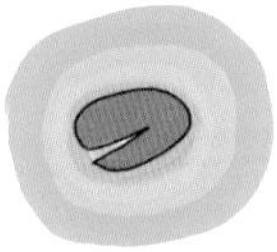

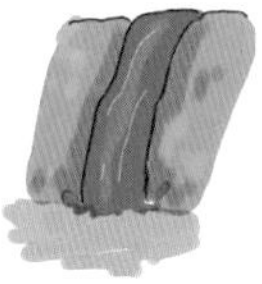

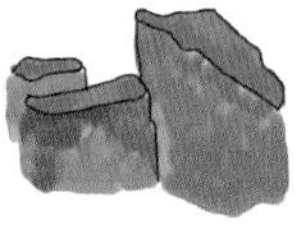

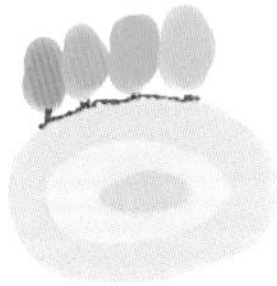

DAY 57

# 도시 건축물

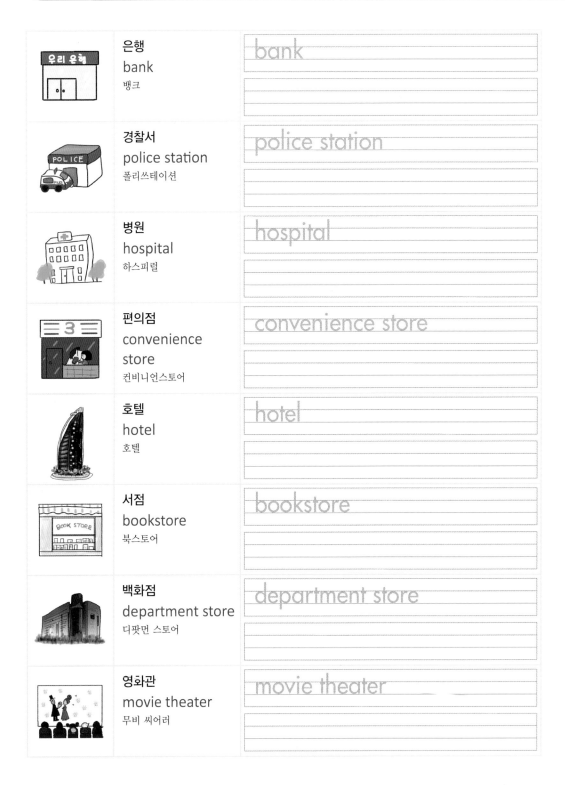

| | | |
|---|---|---|
| | 은행<br>bank<br>뱅크 | bank |
| | 경찰서<br>police station<br>폴리쓰테이션 | police station |
| | 병원<br>hospital<br>하스피럴 | hospital |
| | 편의점<br>convenience store<br>컨비니언스토어 | convenience store |
| | 호텔<br>hotel<br>호텔 | hotel |
| | 서점<br>bookstore<br>북스토어 | bookstore |
| | 백화점<br>department store<br>디팟먼 스토어 | department store |
| | 영화관<br>movie theater<br>무비 씨어러 | movie theater |

| | | |
|---|---|---|
|  | 문구점<br>stationery store<br>스테이셔너리 스토어 | stationery store |
|  | 놀이공원<br>amusement park<br>어뮤즈먼트 파크 | amusement park |
|  | 학교<br>school<br>스쿨 | school |
|  | 공원<br>park<br>파크 | park |
|  | 식물원<br>botanical garden<br>버테니컬 가든 | botanical garden |
|  | 동물원<br>zoo<br>주 | zoo |
|  | 박물관<br>museum<br>뮤지엄 | museum |
|  | 도서관<br>library<br>라이브러리 | library |

DAY 58

# 운동

| | | |
|---|---|---|
|  | 볼링<br>bowling<br>보울링 | bowling |
|  | 테니스<br>tennis<br>테니스 | tennis |
|  | 스키<br>ski<br>스키 | ski |
|  | 축구<br>soccer<br>싸커 | soccer |
|  | 배구<br>volleyball<br>발리볼 | volleyball |
|  | 야구<br>baseball<br>베이스볼 | baseball |
|  | 농구<br>basketball<br>배스킷볼 | basketball |
|  | 닥구<br>table tennis<br>테이블 테니스 | table tennis |

|  |  |  |  |
|---|---|---|---|
| 수영 | swimming | 스위밍 | swimming |
| 배드민턴 | badminton | 배드민튼 | badminton |
| 럭비 | rugby | 럭비 | rugby |
| 스쿼시 | squash | 스쿼쉬 | squash |
| 아이스하키 | ice hockey | 아이스 하키 | ice hockey |
| 핸드볼 | handball | 핸드볼 | handball |
| 피겨스케이팅 | figure skating | 피겨 스케이링 | figure skating |
| 양궁 | archery | 아처리 | archery |

DAY 59

# 오락, 취미

| | | |
|---|---|---|
|  | 영화 감상<br>watching movies<br>와칭 무비스 | watching movies |
|  | 음악 감상<br>listening to music<br>리스닝 투 뮤직 | listening to music |
|  | 여행<br>travel<br>트래블 | travel |
|  | 독서<br>reading<br>리딩 | reading |
|  | 춤추기<br>dancing<br>댄씽 | dancing |
|  | 노래 부르기<br>singing<br>씽잉 | singing |
|  | 운동<br>exercise<br>엑써싸이즈 | exercise |
|  | 등산<br>hiking<br>하이킹 | hiking |

| | | |
|---|---|---|
|  | 악기 연주<br>playing a musical instrument<br>플레잉 어 뮤지컬 인스트러먼트 | playing a musical instrument |
|  | 요리<br>cooking<br>쿠킹 | cooking |
|  | 사진 찍기<br>taking pictures<br>테이킹 픽처스 | taking pictures |
| 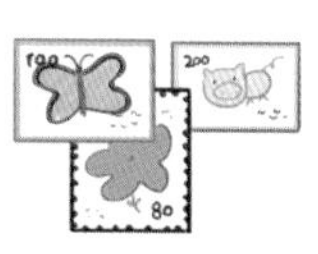 | 우표 수집<br>stamp collecting<br>스탬프 컬렉팅 | stamp collecting |
|  | 십자수<br>cross-stitch<br>크로스티취 | cross-stitch |
|  | TV 보기<br>watching TV<br>와칭 티비 | watching TV |
|  | 인터넷<br>surfing the Internet<br>서핑 디 이너넷 | surfing the Internet |
|  | 뜨개질<br>knitting<br>니딩 | knitting |

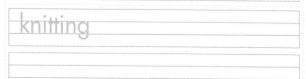

DAY 60

# 악기

| | | |
|---|---|---|
| | 기타<br>guitar<br>기타 | guitar |
| | 피아노<br>piano<br>피애노 | piano |
| | 색소폰<br>saxophone<br>쌕써폰 | saxophone |
| | 플루트<br>flute<br>플룻 | flute |
| | 하모니카<br>harmonica<br>하마니커 | harmonica |
| | 클라리넷<br>clarinet<br>클래러넷 | clarinet |
| | 트럼펫<br>trumpet<br>트럼핏 | trumpet |
| | 하프<br>harp<br>하프 | harp |

| | | |
|---|---|---|
|  | 첼로<br>cello<br>첼로 | cello |
|  | 아코디언<br>accordion<br>어코디언 | accordion |
|  | 드럼<br>drum<br>드럼 | drum |
| 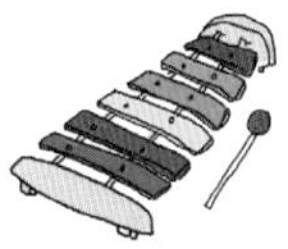 | 실로폰<br>xylophone<br>자일러폰 | xylophone |
|  | 리코더<br>recorder<br>리코더 | recorder |
| 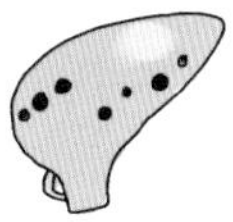 | 오카리나<br>ocarina<br>아커리나 | ocarina |
|  | 바이올린<br>violin<br>바이얼린 | violin |
|  | 비올라<br>viola<br>비얼라 | viola |

## 연습문제A

영어단어에 알맞은 뜻을 연결해 보세요.

| | |
|---|---|
| 1. bank • | • ⓐ 병원 |
| 2. mountain • | • ⓑ 도서관 |
| 3. hospital • | • ⓒ 은행 |
| 4. library • | • ⓓ 공원 |
| 5. river • | • ⓔ 박물관 |
| 6. school • | • ⓕ 산 |
| 7. sea • | • ⓖ 학교 |
| 8. park • | • ⓗ 해안 |
| 9. museum • | • ⓘ 강 |
| 10. island • | • ⓙ 바다 |
| 11. tree • | • ⓚ 연못 |
| 12. coast • | • ⓛ 사막 |
| 13. desert • | • ⓜ 호수 |
| 14. zoo • | • ⓝ 섬 |
| 15. lake • | • ⓞ 동물원 |
| 16. pond • | • ⓟ 나무 |

답 1.ⓒ 2.ⓕ 3.ⓐ 4.ⓑ 5.ⓘ 6.ⓖ 7.ⓙ 8.ⓓ 9.ⓔ 10.ⓝ 11.ⓟ 12.ⓗ 13.ⓛ 14.ⓞ 15.ⓜ 16.ⓚ

## 연습문제B

취미가 무엇인지 우리말 뜻을 보고 밑줄 친 부분에 해당되는 영어 단어를 적어 보세요.

1. 저는 축구를 좋아해요.
   (            )

2. 저는 야구 보는 걸 좋아해요.
   (            )

3. 제 취미는 독서예요.
   (            )

4. 저는 영화 감상을 좋아합니다.
   (                        )

5. 저는 종종 피아노를 쳐요.
   (            )

6. 제 취미는 바이올린을 연주하는 것입니다.
   (            )

7. 제 취미는 춤추기예요.
   (            )

8. 저는 동생과 배드민턴을 치는 것이 취미입니다.
   (            )

9. 저는 방과 후에 친구들과 농구를 종종 합니다.
   (            )

10. 저는 TV 프로그램을 보고 요리를 따라 하는 것이 재미있어요.
    (            )

답 1. soccer 2. baseball 3. reading 4. watching movies 5. piano 6. violin 7. dancing 8. badminton 9. basketball 10. cooking

MEMO